Nemesis of the Great

Cinzi Lavin

Nemesis of the Great is a work of fiction. Names, characters, events and incidents are the products of the author's imagination. Any resemblance to actual persons, living or dead, or actual events is purely coincidental.

Cover art: Neyret Freres weaving "Deer in The Forest Twilight" by Rosa Bonheur

ISBN: 978-1-7366350-1-8

To John Kenneth Galbraith

for being able to see it coming

PART ONE

Air-conducting "O Fortuna" was one of Bryce's favorite things. He wasn't musical, but something about the grandiosity of the piece inspired his artistic side. He loved the majestic opening, the delicately rhythmic melody, and especially the thrilling climb to the booming conclusion.

He was at his cabin in Norfolk, Connecticut and luckily, didn't have to worry about disturbing his neighbors, who were several dozen acres away. Money was good for buying privacy, time, and options.

However, he was running short on time at the moment. He knew he should be leaving soon to attend the christening of his niece in New York. It was a chilly Sunday morning.

He was in fine spirits, which is why he'd exuberantly chosen a loud classical piece to set the tone for the day, like on Easter mornings, when he played "Ye Choirs of New Jerusalem" at thunderous decibels.

After checking his tie and retrieving his christening gift from the table by the door, he sped off to Tuxedo Park. The small white box with the pink ribbon that sat on the passenger seat contained a silver rattle inscribed with the baby's name and birthdate.

Bryce was a little surprised that his sister Susan had chosen to baptize the baby so young. Susan and her wife, Patty, had adopted the newborn a few weeks previously and this would be the child's first official presentation. Patty's parents and brothers had come from King of Prussia, Pennsylvania. Friends and family would be in attendance. Generally, Episcopalians waited until the child had adjusted to life ex-utero and had cultivated a normal appearance; it also gave the mother time to reclaim her figure. Meanwhile, Catholics raced their babies to the altar, practically still red and wrinkly, to save their souls lest they die unchristened and wind up in Limbo. While the Catholic babies were possibly on safer spiritual footing, Episcopalian babies looked so much better in photos.

At any rate, Bryce had been honored to have been chosen as the baby's godfather. After a life of relative ignominy, he was suddenly feeling very ceremonial, having been the one to give away his longtime friend, Nathalie, at her recent wedding in August at the same church where the christening was taking place. As it so happened, Nathalie was to be the godmother. She and her husband, Ben, lived next door to Susan and Patty, so she would be able to spend a lot of time with the baby.

Bryce wondered at first why they didn't choose one of Patty's three brothers to be the godfather, but Patty had explained to him that they were all older than she and already had children of their own. She and Susan thought a set of young godparents would be nice.

He mused about the significance of his role. Technically, it meant that if anything happened to Susan and Patty, he and Nathalie would be responsible for raising the child, although in reality, that responsibility would probably fall on Patty's parents, since they were the only living grandparents. Bryce and Susan had been orphaned some years back by the death of their mother, their father having also died previously. As a bachelor, Bryce didn't see himself as ideal father material, although there was no question in his mind that Nathalie would make an amazing mother. Considering her husband Ben—whom Bryce also imagined would make an outstanding father—was rolling in money, the child would surely want for nothing. Nathalie's family was rich, but Ben came from big Chinese money. He owned a jet.

Bryce was continually amused how the poor and middle-class lumped the rich together into one all-inclusive category when there were very important stratifications of wealth to which they were clearly oblivious. As soon as they saw a Mercedes or a big diamond engagement ring, they decided the person was "rich," not realizing that the Mercedes could be a lease, or the ring could have been bought on credit. Bryce knew better. Owning a jet, an island, or controlling interest in a corporation was *rich*. He and his family were merely comfortably well off.

It also amused him (and frequently disgusted him) that the *nouveau riche* were commonly considered sophisticates by those who didn't know any better, whereas Old Money people such as himself found them tacky and gaudy in the extreme. They had piles of money but no class whatsoever. They owned jets and islands and would probably buy the Grand Canyon if they could. He could easily see them turning it into a giant hot tub. You could always tell new money because they owned hot tubs. Bryce shuddered involuntarily.

When Bryce arrived at the church, he stared a moment at the grand stone structure. It was not the church in which he himself had been christened. He had been raised in Ardsley in Westchester County, on the other side of the Hudson River. The house in Tuxedo Park was the one in which his mother had grown up. Susan and Patty had been given it as a wedding present, and Susan, who was now the head of the family since Grandfather's death, was establishing her line there.

Meanwhile, Bryce had settled permanently in the cottage that had been Grandfather's in Norfolk. He would've liked to have had it willed to him, but it had actually been left to Susan. To Bryce, Grandfather had left nothing. Susan had chosen to give it to him, along with other holdings. Apparently, Grandfather had been horribly disappointed in Bryce for having disentangled himself from the strings which came attached to his family fortune and having struck it out on his own shortly after starting college. As a consequence of rejecting family money, he was unable to afford to finish his education and worked a string of writing and teaching jobs, often for minimal pay. It had been hard, and while he felt sure of his principles, there was something bitter about it as well. The realization that those who played by the rules were richly rewarded—regardless of how deserving or undeserving they might be—struck a sharp contrast to the desolation experienced by someone who followed their conscience. Then again, Bryce remembered a saying of his father's, "Virtue is its own reward."

At least he could look himself in the mirror. He'd held true to his ideals, even causing a scandal by breaking his engagement earlier that year with Claudia Burkle, the daughter of a prominent

European manufacturer. He'd found her bland, despite family pressure to marry her. The only thing that had saved him socially was Nathalie's choice to have him give her away at her wedding. Her wealth and influence was the rubber-stamp of approval that kept him on people's dinner guest and Christmas card lists. Not only did the invitations not stop coming, they increased. Becoming the godfather of Susan's baby was also hardly incidental. With a small fortune of his own and the beaming approval of powerful figures, he was once again a member of society. He had to admit it felt good.

He strode into the church. There were Susan and Patty talking to the priest. Bryce was glad to see it was Father Jeff. He was young and new, and he'd been the one who performed Nathalie and Ben's marriage.

Father Jeff had a lively sense of humor. He knew how to strike the perfect balance between comedy and diplomacy. Bryce remembered his announcement one Sunday regarding the issue of an extensive roof repair which the congregation was facing. He said he had pored over the estimates from the construction company as well as the church's finances.

"The good news," he'd reported, "is that we have all the money we need to cover the necessary repairs. The bad news is that it's all in your wallets."

After a startled pause, the congregants began to laugh lightly. There was a reason Episcopalians were jokingly known as "God's frozen people."

Father Jeff was from somewhere in the Midwest. Bryce wondered how he'd managed to wind up at such an elite congregation. Probably the search committee had been striving for someone with fresh enthusiasm and a certain informality conducive to a congenial church atmosphere. The old pastor, Father Peter, had been a real stone-faced hardliner. He'd married Bryce's parents. A lot of the old folks liked him, but they slowly warmed to Father Jeff. He had a certain youthful appeal that was hard to resist. And he might have come from the sticks, but you could tell he had half a brain.

As Bryce approached the altar, Father Jeff called out to him.

"Bryce! Good to see you!"

"Good morning, Father Jeff," Bryce said.

"Please—call me Jeff," the priest said. Bryce knew it was what Father Jeff preferred, but still, it felt like it was going a little too far. After all, he was a man of the cloth, not a plumber.

As Bryce approached, he saw Nathalie and Ben sitting in a front pew. Nathalie was holding the baby, who was sitting up and smiling.

"Our star attraction this morning seems to be in good form," Father Jeff said.

"I just hope she won't start fussing during Mass," Susan said.

"Well," said Father Jeff, "Babies sometimes do, but that's perfectly okay. They haven't learned yet how to pretend my sermons aren't boring. Give her time."

"Good morning, Bryce," said Nathalie and Ben, almost in unison.

"Oh! Her sock!" exclaimed Patty in dismay, reaching down to pull the baby's sock out of her shoe, where it had slithered.

"Now if I can just keep Patty from fussing over the baby," said Susan, obviously irritated.

Father Jeff laughed. "All new parents have Christening Anxiety. I promise everything will be fine." He looked at Bryce and Nathalie. "You two ready to go?"

"Yes," they both said.

"Good," said Father Jeff. "In that case, we can take a break and Mass will start shortly. I'll cue you when it's time to come up for the baptism, so try not to fall asleep." He paused. "But before I step away, I would like us to join for a moment of prayer right now."

Everyone rose. Father Jeff said a few words asking for God's blessing on the baby and on the family, and offering gratitude for the spirit of love that caused the occasion. It was a sweet prayer, delivered with obvious sincerity.

When they were finished, Father Jeff looked at everyone. "We good?" he asked.

Everyone nodded yes.

"Great. Then let's lock and load!"

With that, Father Jeff turned heel and walked briskly to his office and everyone else got settled in the front pews on the left side where the baptismal font was located. The organist had come in and was warming up. Soon Aunt Bitsy arrived. She greeted Susan and Patty and made much over the baby, who started squirming at the sound of the organ's low tones.

Aunt Bitsy had been the best friend of Susan and Bryce's mother and had basically filled her place for them ever since at formal affairs and functions. She'd orchestrated the ill-fated match between Bryce and Claudia with the best of intentions, and while Bryce knew he'd disappointed her, in true motherly fashion, she continued to champion him every chance she got. Her own daughter, Pamela, had died in a car accident years ago, and she was also a widow, so Susan and Bryce meant a lot to her.

Next came Ingrid Masterson, Nathalie's mother. Ingrid's husband, Minty, had died earlier in the year. She'd decided to give the house to Nathalie and Ben, since it was where Nathalie had lived all her life. She'd spent the last several months away on Viking Ocean Cruises. She hadn't yet decided where she was going to live.

Members of the congregation started coming in and soon the church was abuzz with excited whispers. Patty's family, the Robinsons, arrived. Some of Susan's college friends crept up to say a quick hello before claiming their seats. Everyone petted the baby and Patty kept fastidiously adjusting her socks. The sun was beaming through the stained-glass window next to them and Bryce thought it made a lovely atmosphere.

Uncle Clement and Aunt Fluff arrived and seated themselves in the front pew with the christening party. Uncle Clement was Grandfather's younger brother, the oldest representative of the Parnell side. His wife, Fluff, was a cloying woman whom Bryce disliked. At one point back when there had been the prospect of Susan and Patty adopting a boy and they were discussing possible Biblical names, Aunt Fluff had said "Whatever you do, don't name him Jesus or people will think you're Puerto Ricans."

Just then, as Bryce turned to get a mint out of his pocket, he caught sight of something strange out of the corner of his eye. Going against his childhood teachings on church etiquette, he looked directly behind him and saw a tall, powerfully built man approaching. He had a shock of platinum blonde hair, a high-fashion suit that appeared to be mauve in color, and he was wearing sunglasses.

Who wears sunglasses in church? thought Bryce.

The man strode up to Patty, who immediately leapt from her seat and embraced him.

"Gabe!" she cried.

"Where's the princess?" he asked, after Patty released him. Then he spotted the baby and, taking her from Nathalie, swung her up into the air and tossed her playfully overhead.

Bryce was aghast. Mass was about to start any moment and here this man made a celebrity entrance and was tossing the baby around like a cabbage.

Ben leaned over to him and whispered "He's a friend of Patty's."

That figured. Patty was an artist—a photographer—and she knew some pretty unconventional people. This Gabe definitely fit the bill. Bryce wondered how Ben knew this, but in the year since he'd met Ben, he'd come to realize that Ben had a knack for finding out all kinds of things, which was particularly impressive considering he was from a foreign country. Bryce figured if he himself ever moved abroad, he'd be clueless most of the time.

Uncle Clement coughed noticeably on purpose, and everyone realized that the choir had begun processing down the aisle. Gabe vanished somewhere into the back of the sanctuary.

The Mass was very nice. The sermon turned out not to be particularly boring at all, although Bryce wasn't mad about the reading. It was a letter from St. Paul, an exhortation to some new church. It seemed to Bryce there were a lot of those letters in the Bible, exhortations from St. Paul about something or other. Bryce imagined St. Paul must've gone around exhorting constantly.

When the time came for the christening, the baby was as good as gold. She smiled on cue. Tears rolled down Patty's cheeks as she clasped her hands in front of her, watching Father Jeff hold her daughter over the font and anoint her. Susan glowed with pride, and when the priest intoned the baby's name, Alexandra Elizabeth, everyone knew that she was now an official member of the family of God, but more importantly, of the Robinson-Parnells.

2

"How ever did you come up with such a lovely name?" Aunt Bitsy asked, when they'd arrived back at Susan and Patty's house, as she enthusiastically munched a broiled canapé made of a mixture of cream cheese, egg yolks, and grated onions. It was one of the specialties of their maid, Margaret. In all other respects, Aunt Bitsy was the model of good breeding but she sometimes found herself unable to exercise restraint around food. She'd already polished off half a dozen.

Susan fielded the question. She explained that they both wanted something classic yet commanding, and Patty leaned towards something poetic, so they settled on the combination of two queenly names. Patty chimed in to add that the baby's nickname would be "Sandy." She liked the informality of it. Susan didn't say anything, but Bryce knew his sister well enough to know she'd always call her daughter "Alexandra."

Nathalie was holding the baby. She'd been changed out of her heirloom christening gown, the one in which he and Susan and countless other Parnells had been baptized. She was now wearing a frothy white party dress, a gift from Patty's mother. She looked like a bon-bon. Bryce realized she really was an adorable baby. Nathalie caught Bryce's eye and came over.

"The Jorgensens are here and I'd like to go have a word with them," she said. "Do you mind taking her?"

Bryce didn't consider himself great with children, but he figured that as Sandy's godfather, he should give it a shot.

"Sure," he said, setting down his drink on an end-table and cradling the baby in his arms.

Holding a baby always made him feel like sitting so that in case of dropping, there wouldn't be as far to fall, but everyone seemed to be adept at walking around with a baby, so he tried. It felt awkward. It strained his arms, and the baby squiggled uncomfortably.

He realized the problem was that the child was in a prone position. He hoisted her up so that she was sitting on his forearm at the crook of his elbow and he put his other hand on her shoulder to keep her from tumbling off. That seemed to work better and she looked happy to be able to see what was going on around her.

Considering the house was filled with people, there was plenty to take in.

"So that's what you want," Bryce said to her. "You want to greet all your guests."

He turned her in the direction to which Nathalie had gone.

"There's your godmother," he said, reassuring the child. "She's talking to the Jorgensens. Aris and Loretta. See? They're in-laws of your Grandma Parnell. They're intellectuals. They're very smart. Loretta's the retired dean of a Seven Sisters college where I bet Susan's going to send you when you grow up."

Sandy clasped Bryce's index finger and looked wonderingly at his face.

“Who wants to go to a Seven Sisters college? Yes, you!” he said, wiggling his finger. She smiled.

Bryce had to admit she was a good-natured baby. She had a faint growth of light brown hair and big blue eyes. She resembled Susan a little. Bryce wasn’t surprised that they were able to adopt a baby so quickly. Susan’s lawyers had arranged everything. Bryce didn’t ask any questions but he had a feeling they found an unfit young mother and got her to turn over parental rights in exchange for a lot of money and a promise never to try contacting the child.

Bryce realized it was a good thing Sandy had been adopted by his sister, or she might’ve wound up living in a trailer park somewhere. Tuxedo Park was definitely better. Besides, once Nathalie and Ben started a family, Sandy would have little neighbor-children with whom to play.

Sandy turned towards the buffet, dazzled by all the colorful foods.

“Look at what we have here!” Bryce said animatedly. “There’s fruit and cheese and olives and crackers. We have crudités and pickles and quiche and potato salad and sliced cold cuts and some nice fresh rolls. And here we have deviled eggs and spinach dip and—”

Just then, Margaret’s son John came out of the kitchen. He had come today to help his mother. He set a tray of stuffed mushrooms on the table.

“Hi John,” Bryce said.

“Hello,” John said, coming to shake Bryce’s hand. “I hear the christening went well.”

“Yes,” Bryce replied. “I don’t think you’ve met my goddaughter, Alexandra.”

“Pleased to meet you, Alexandra,” said John, smiling. He was an exceptionally plain-looking lad, but he had a nice smile.

“How are things at Fordham?” Bryce asked. John was starting his second year of law school. Susan was paying half of his tuition and expenses.

“Great,” John said. “I took summer courses, so by my third year I’ll have a lighter schedule.” John explained that he was also working part-time at a law firm.

Bryce, who’d never made it to the end of his freshman year at an Ivy League school, was highly impressed.

John wrinkled his nose and looked at the baby. “I think she needs to be changed,” he said.

“This *is* her party dress,” Bryce explained. “They’ve already changed her out of the christening gown.” John was Catholic, so Bryce assumed he thought the fancy white party dress was what she’d worn during the ceremony, not realizing that Episcopalian babies often sported highly ornate lace gowns. Bryce figured someone of John’s lower social standing would probably think she should be changed into play clothes.

“No,” said John, “I mean her diaper.”

"Oh," said Bryce. He had no idea what to do about that.

"Here, I'll take her," said John, sensing Bryce's confusion.

"You know how to change diapers?" Bryce asked in surprise.

"No, but my mom does," John said, disappearing into the kitchen. Margaret would take care of it, Bryce realized. She knew how to do everything.

Bryce went to retrieve his drink in the sitting room. It was then that he saw Patty's friend, Gabe, arrive.

3

Gabe entered the house and didn't remove his sunglasses. Clearly, it was some kind of style thing. He probably slept with them on.

Margaret, who'd opened the door for him, gave one of her famous disapproving looks behind his back. She wasn't a talkative woman and even though she was of Irish extraction, she was living proof of the Amish saying "Why waste words when a look will do?"

Bryce couldn't tell if Gabe were from San Francisco or Barcelona. There was something European about his flair, but at the same time it had a certain edginess to it. He walked in like he owned the place and went straight to Patty.

"Pattycakes!" he said, giving her an enormous hug and then, lifting her off her feet, he swirled her around. Patty was jubilant.

Why does this guy feel the need to manhandle everyone? Bryce wondered. Maybe he used to be a bouncer for a tony New York nightclub. That was a possibility. He was certainly big enough.

"Is that suit mauve, or is it me?" whispered Aunt Bitsy, who was standing nearby.

"Yes, I think it is," said Bryce. "He's some friend of Patty's."

"He's a ne'er-do-well, if ever I saw one," she said. Aunt Bitsy's vocabulary hadn't been updated since the Roosevelt administration.

Patty began introducing Gabe around. It appeared Susan was meeting him for the first time.

Bryce was no detective, but he began to reason that Gabe had probably flown in from somewhere. Patty had probably told Nathalie and Ben that Gabe was coming, which was probably how Ben knew about it. Gabe didn't appear to have an accent, so it was likely he was American. Perhaps he was a fellow artist.

Gabe had begun chatting with Nathalie and Ben, and one of Patty's brothers joined them. Her brothers all had names starting with "J," and Bryce could never keep them straight. Joe? Jack? James? It didn't help that they all looked very similar, too.

Before he knew it, Aris and Loretta Jorgensen were on the spot, introducing themselves to Gabe. They loved meeting anyone new and learning whatever they could.

Bryce wasn't eager to meet Gabe, so he headed in the opposite direction. Uncle Clement was seated on that side of the room and Aunt Fluff wasn't around, so Bryce was happy to sit and chat.

"How much do you think his suit's worth?" Bryce asked him. Uncle Clement could gauge the price of just about anything. It was astonishing.

"Not as much as he'd like you to think it's worth. It's all in the way he carries himself," he replied.

"It almost has a sheen to it," Bryce said, studying it from afar. "It reminds me of those new suits that are waterproof. Those are pretty pricey."

"That's the most ridiculous thing I've ever heard of," Uncle Clement said. "What damned fool would pay good money for a waterproof suit when he can buy an umbrella? I don't know what's become of this world."

Bryce laughed. Uncle Clement reminded him of Grandfather, or rather the man Grandfather could've been if he hadn't been so stern.

"Now the one thing that makes a suit like that valuable," he said, leaning towards Bryce, "is that a stylish man is always a hit with the ladies."

"Oh," said Bryce, "then you don't think he's—"

"Nah," replied Uncle Clement. "I saw him getting a girl's phone number when we were at the church. She looked like a hot ticket, if you know what I mean."

"Have you been golfing lately?" asked Bryce.

"Not for a while. Not feeling up to it," Uncle Clement explained. He'd been feeling poorly since Grandfather's death a year ago. "Did I ever tell you how I learned to play?" he asked Bryce.

Bryce said that he had not.

"I learned with hickory clubs. That's what my father used. Now that'll make a real golfer of you. You have to develop skill to use them, not like these modern clubs." He paused a moment. "I still have my father's best set, but I don't have any more use for them. I'll bring them for you next time."

Bryce was touched. Uncle Clement and Aunt Fluff didn't have any children. All of their generosity was directed at Aunt Fluff's sister's children. Bryce figured the golf clubs were the only pass-down he'd ever receive from them, and even then, probably only because Uncle Clement was convinced he was going to die soon and he knew those clubs would wind up with Aunt Fluff's great-nephew if he didn't give them to Bryce now. He was grateful, but it stung a little that his great-uncle was showing more consideration of him than his own grandfather had. Grandfather hadn't left him so much as a matchstick.

Aunt Fluff was approaching. Bryce got up to leave, making an excuse about having to check on something. He was happy to see that Monsignor Ryan had arrived, so he went to greet him.

"Where's Marguerite?" Bryce asked, inquiring after his wife.

"She's home with a cold or allergies. She can't tell which. There's a lot of mold this time of year and it always gets to her," he replied.

Monsignor Ryan was an old friend of his father's who'd earned his nickname as the result of a remark inquiring about a restaurant's clergy discount.

"And where is the baby?" Monsignor Ryan asked, smiling. "I didn't come all this way just to see the same old faces, you know."

Bryce looked around. Margaret had changed Sandy's diaper and returned her to Patty, who was handing her off to Susan because she was still paying rapt attention to Gabe.

"Susan has her," Bryce said.

"Well, aren't you going to introduce me?" Monsignor Ryan joked.

Bryce was happy to do the honors, but it would mean getting within spitting distance of Gabe, and Bryce still wasn't sure what to make of him.

They crossed the room and Monsignor Ryan held out his finger for Sandy, who grabbed it and looked into his face.

"That's your Grandad Parnell's friend," Susan told her. Sandy smiled.

"Look at those blue eyes," Monsignor Ryan said. "She's going to have all the boys after her." Then an awkward look crossed his face and he quickly added "Or girls."

Susan laughed. She rarely did, but when she did, it was a hearty, wholesome laugh.

"It's okay, Ned. Chances are she'll probably be straight," Susan explained.

"Well, you know, I didn't want to—" he began, but Susan cut him off.

"No worries. But whatever she is, I should probably have Margaret put her down for a nap." She began scanning the room for Margaret. "She's had a big morning and I don't want her up all afternoon partying like a rock star. She's had enough exposure for one day."

Monsignor Ryan excused himself to get a drink, and Susan caught Margaret's eye. After Sandy had been whisked off for her nap, Bryce said, "Speaking of rock stars, what's with Gabe?"

"Friend of Patty's," Susan answered, taking a sip of champagne. "They met because he's a fan of her work. He buys tons of her prints and he's the one who got her introduced to several really important galleries in Europe."

"Where's he from?" he asked.

Susan looked at him with a raised eyebrow. "That's . . . interesting," she explained. She went on to tell him that Gabe's family was Old Money from Duxbury, Massachusetts. Not Mayflower Society old, but old enough. There was some Irish in the family line. Due to various misfortunes, the family had thinned out to the point that Gabe's was the only one left, but they still had plenty of money, or so they thought until one day when the father quite literally left to get a pack of cigarettes and never returned.

"He'd gambled it all and left a ton of debt," Susan said.

"What happened then?" Bryce asked.

Susan told him the mother had to get a menial job and they had to move into a tiny apartment in South Boston where she had some distant Irish relations who sometimes helped looking after the children. Gabe and his siblings had a rough childhood, often living on welfare. Gabe had put himself through college and become an economist.

So that explained why Bryce couldn't place him: he was a Bostonian. Any time he met someone who was strange in a way he couldn't quite figure out, they were inevitably from Boston.

"You two have a lot in common," Susan added. Bryce couldn't fathom how that could be, but she said "He's a man of the people with soulful eyes."

"Is that why he never takes those sunglasses off?" Bryce asked. Susan laughed.

She said "He's always on some bleeding-heart campaign to save the poor."

At that point, Patty approached them with Gabe in tow.

"Bryce," she said, "This is Gabe, a dear, dear friend of mine." Turning to Gabe she said, "This is Susan's brother, Bryce." They shook hands. Bryce was pleasantly surprised that he wasn't given a bone-crushing handshake, which is usually what big guys did. He did, however, notice that Gabe was wearing a cologne with which he wasn't familiar but which he guessed was very expensive.

"Patty says you're starting a non-profit. I'd be very interested to hear all about it," he said.

Bryce hated being put on the spot like that. This was a social function, not a business meeting.

He brushed it off and made some vague comments about how he had just started it and still had a lot to learn.

"For Patty's brother-in-law, I'd be happy to do anything I can," Gabe boldly said, adding, "Seriously, give me a call. I could do a lot for you." He explained that he'd flown in from Sweden last night and would be in the area for the next few months. He handed Bryce his business card.

Gabe then turned to Susan and said in a mock-chiding tone, "You should've gone for the harp."

Susan didn't miss a beat, replying "Not for that price, I shouldn't've."

"Harp?" Bryce asked.

Patty explained. "I wanted to hire a harpist to play for the party but Susan said it was too expensive."

Susan said, "Do you have any idea what they charge? I could've hired a small orchestra for the same price!"

"What's wrong with someone wanting to get paid for their services?" Gabe asked.

"Nothing," Susan replied, "Only she was asking too much."

"That's subjective," said Gabe. "Anything is only ever worth what someone is willing to pay for it. Supply and demand." He smiled a mischievous smile. Bryce realized that watching an economist try to take his sister down would be interesting.

"Her fee was outrageous," Susan said flatly. "She must not want anyone to hire her, I'll say that."

"On the contrary," Gabe pointed out, "She's clearly successful at getting hired at that price or she wouldn't charge it."

"I don't believe it," replied Susan.

Gabe continued. "She spent years paying for harp lessons, thousands of hours practicing, and then even more years gaining a professional reputation as a competent, reliable performer."

Susan was shaking her head. "What she was charging was robbery."

Gabe took another tack. "Okay. Let's pretend you're the harpist. You have transportation costs to and from the venue. Strings have to be replaced occasionally. You're an independent contractor so you don't have health insurance. And then, of course, there's rent, bills, and food, not to mention recouping something for all those years of lessons. How much are you going to charge?"

Susan said, "I'd probably be asking five times what she's asking, but that's not the point."

"It's not the point that someone's trying to make a living by performing a valuable skill?" he asked. "Then what *is* the point?"

"The point is that people like that make their own choices. It's not my fault she can't support herself without charging exorbitant prices and I'm not going to subsidize that kind of lifestyle. She's just another artist with her head in the clouds like this one," Susan said, indicating Patty.

"But what if you were her friend?" Gabe asked, undeterred by Susan's evasion. "Better yet, what if you were her mother? What if Sandy grows up to be a harpist? How much would you tell her to charge?"

Susan frowned at him. "I can see you're trying to make this personal," she said.

"Because it *is* personal," Gabe said. He moved his hand between them. "*We* are *persons*. We have to learn how to do things for our mutual benefit. You can easily afford her fee. So you hire the harpist. She pays the grocer. The grocer pays taxes for his children to go to school. It's all connected."

Susan looked frustrated. She said, "I don't know what kind of communism you're trying to sell me, but I'm not buying that, either."

Gabe threw his head back and laughed so loudly that people turned to stare.

"I told you she was tough," Patty said to Gabe.

Gabe leaned forward and startled Susan by grabbing her by the shoulders and giving her a big kiss on the cheek.

"Well, I love her anyway, because she loves my Pattycakes," he said, adding, "Where's the champagne?"

After Gabe and Patty were gone, Bryce remembered he had Gabe's card in his hand. He looked at it. It read "Malcolm Gabriel Mills, Economist" and included a phone number. He tucked it in his pocket.

By the end of the afternoon after the coffee and cake had been served, people started to leave. Patty came over and sat beside Bryce. She looked happy but exhausted.

"I'm sorry I haven't talked to you all day but it's been so hectic," she said. "Did you enjoy the cake?"

"Yes," Bryce said. "It was fantastic."

"Good," Patty said, nodding. "Margaret recommended this new German bakery to us and I was hoping it would be good." She continued, "I want you to know how proud I am to have you as Sandy's godfather."

"This is all new for me, but I'll do my best," Bryce said.

"That's all it is," Patty said. "I want my daughter to grow up with people around her who love her and care about her. That's so important. And Susan wants her to have a very conventional life, but I want her to know all kinds of people. Promise me you'll show her that there's a bigger world than this, because I know you know it exists."

Bryce was somewhat surprised by her request. He gathered that she thought him a man of broad experience because he'd broken away from the family for a time. Before he could respond, it was as if Patty had read his thoughts.

"Even though I'm an artist, I've never really stepped outside the magic circle. If I'm honest with myself, it's because I didn't have the courage. But I know that you do. That's what I want Sandy to have."

"I promise to try," he told her.

Patty gave him a big hug and said she had to go look for Margaret, but added, "And do call Gabe. He's really something. You'll see."

4

The following day, Bryce found himself knocking at the door of Tiffany's new apartment. Tiffany was the fiancée of his friend Deek, and they had invited him to lunch. It was all part of an elaborate plan to acclimate Tiffany to the kind of life she would be leading as the wife of an extremely wealthy heir from Hilton Head, South Carolina.

Deek and Tiffany had planned a long engagement to give Tiffany enough time to learn what she'd need to in order to survive in her new social circle, considering she came from humble beginnings.

The lunch was a chance for her to play hostess in her own environment and Bryce was there to be her "practice" guest. She'd previously lived in some wretched hole in Co-op City, but Deek got her a simple yet elegant place in Eastchester. It was still a slightly seedy town around the edges, so she wouldn't get completely homesick, yet close enough to affluent communities, such as Scarsdale, to give her a taste of better things.

Tiffany answered the door.

"Bryce," said the chubby redhead with a smile, "I'm so glad to see you. Please come in." Then she turned to Deek, who was standing several paces back and asked "How's that?"

"That was just fine; very good," Deek said.

Bryce was impressed. He could hardly believe this was the same woman who, just a few short months ago, had been ejected from a Newport Creamery in Rhode Island for throwing limes and swearing. That had been a memorable day, Bryce recalled.

He handed her a small bouquet of carnations. He figured they were hardy enough flowers to withstand whatever inept care she might give them, but she seemed to know what to do.

"Thank you," she said. "Please have a seat and I'll put these in a vase." She pronounced "vase" so that it rhymed with "haze."

"*Vase*, honey, *vase*," prompted Deek, pronouncing it so that it rhymed with "bras."

"Kiss my ass," she said, turning and storming off into the kitchen. Clearly, there was still much room for improvement.

"Hey Bryce," said Deek with a tired smile, offering his hand.

"Keep up the good work," Bryce said, giving him an energetic handshake.

"I'll be right out with drinks," Tiffany yelled from the kitchen.

Deek rolled his eyes and walked to the kitchen door. He leaned in and spoke to her.

"We don't yell across the house. Don't talk to someone unless you're in the same room with them," he said.

Tiffany came to the doorway and stood almost nose-to-nose with Deek.

"I'll be right out with the drinks," she said between clenched teeth.

"Much better," Deek praised her.

She went back into the kitchen and Bryce and Deek sat on the couch. Bryce had to admit the apartment was nicely decorated and said so.

"Isn't it, though?" Deek said. "She did this all by herself. She wanted it to be lots of different shades of cream and beige."

Bryce highly doubted that Tiffany knew the word "beige," but he could imagine her pointing at things in a catalogue and saying "I want that." In any event, the effect was quite tasteful.

Within moments, she reappeared with cold drinks on a tray.

"Deacon," she said to Deek, "Would you please pass a coaster to our guest?"

Deek passed a coaster to Bryce, and Bryce said, "Thank you."

When she handed him his drink, Bryce noticed that Tiffany no longer had trashy-looking long, colorful fake nails, but instead her fingertips had been gracefully manicured. She was wearing a pale-colored nail varnish.

"Your nails look lovely," Bryce commented.

"Thank you," Tiffany said. "Less is more."

With that, she returned to the kitchen to prepare to serve.

"Now I know how Henry Higgins felt," Deek sighed.

"What's coming up on the social calendar?" Bryce asked.

"Well, we've got the Habitat for Humanity gala in a couple of weeks. That should be interesting," Deek replied.

"Why did you choose that event?" Bryce asked.

"We talked about different charities and Tiffany felt strongly about people being able to get housing, so we decided to go with that one," Deek said.

"I could see her becoming a very committed charity worker," Bryce said.

Tiffany appeared at the kitchen doorway to invite the men to be seated.

Once they were at the table, she served a green salad and pimiento cheese sandwiches.

"Thank you, Tiffany," Bryce said. "This looks delicious."

"Well, it ain't no Chicken McGangbang, but it's good," she said.

"Now Tiffany, you know better; that's not a fitting subject," Deek began angrily.

"Chicken McGangbang?" Bryce repeated. "What the hell is *that*?"

Then he realized that he was encouraging her and regretted the question. He apologized to Deek, who simply shrugged and said "It's okay, go ahead." One thing about Tiffany that Bryce enjoyed was that she knew all kinds of unseemly things and didn't appear to have an "edit" button like everyone else. It made for some interesting, if unsettling, conversations.

"People like you don't know about the Secret Menus," she said, smiling wickedly.

"What secret menus?" Bryce asked.

Tiffany went on to explain that most fast-food restaurants had unofficial items that weren't on the menu but which could be prepared at special request, particularly if you were being served by someone young and hip.

She was highly amused by Bryce's ignorance of this.

"Stick with me," she said, laughing. "Next time, I'll teach you how to make a Jailhouse Burrito."

Bryce didn't even want to imagine what that might entail.

"Tiffany, I think that's enough," Deek said pleadingly. "Please, let's talk about something else."

"Okay," she said, turning to Bryce. "How's it going with Rosemary?"

"Yes, how is she?" Deek asked, brightening to the topic.

Bryce would've rather discussed Jailhouse Burritos. Rosemary was a woman he'd started dating a few months earlier. She was an employee of Ben's, and they'd met while Bryce was doing some temporary work for the company. Although they'd gotten along great, Rosemary was reluctant to commit because there was another man in the picture, an old flame of hers who was studying to be a priest. It was upsetting to Bryce because he felt the only reason she was with him was because David was unavailable. And what if David should change his mind about the priesthood? Would Rosemary leave him?

"Well, to be honest, we've kind of stalled out," he explained.

Tiffany pinned him with a piercing look. "So you fu—" she started, then caught herself and rephrased "—fudged it up?"

Deek had mentioned something about Tiffany finding it impossible to give up swearing cold turkey, so they'd given her the temporary option of using substitute words like "fudge," "sugar," and so on. The effect was bizarre.

"Well," he replied, "There are some complications with another man."

Deek shook his head. "That's always your problem. Like Leslie chasing after that fellow at work," he said, then he quickly added, "Oh, I'm sorry, I shouldn't have said that."

"It's okay," Bryce assured him.

Leslie had been a woman Bryce had pursued during the past few years, but she was smitten with a married colleague. She was unstable and irrational. She seemed thrilled by the drama of the hopeless situation, which culminated when she found out he was sleeping with someone else and finally took her own life on New Year's Eve. They hadn't been on speaking terms at the time, and Bryce still felt badly about it.

"How'd she do it again?" Tiffany asked.

"We don't ask those kind of questions," Deek admonished. "That's too personal."

"Well, your mother asked me if my parents were married when I was born. That's pretty fudging personal," she countered.

Bryce fought the urge to ask if they were, but realized Deek would probably have a stroke if he did. He was supposed to be helping with Tiffany's tutelage, not descending to her level.

Changing the subject, Bryce offered "Claudia got married. Aunt Bitsy told me she went to Vienna after we broke up and married the one of her father's competitors."

"Smart business move," Deek said.

"I heard he's as old as her father, though," Bryce said.

"Sounds like a perv," Tiffany commented. Deek scowled at her. "Sorry," she said.

Bryce explained, "She was really eager to have children before it was too late, and I guess this guy had always had an eye for her, so that's probably why she did it."

"But you have to admit it was also a pretty masterful move from a business standpoint," Deek said. Bryce could tell that he was growing into the savvy kind of man who was going to be able to manage the financial empire he would someday inherit.

Tiffany shivered. "I wouldn't let a creepy old melon farmer like that touch me."

Bryce was thoroughly puzzled for a moment, but then he got it. These substitute swear-words were extremely awkward. He almost preferred the profanity.

"But anyway, what about Rosemary?" Tiffany asked, nibbling delicately on her sandwich. Bryce could tell she definitely had the eating thing down.

"We're still officially going out but we haven't been seeing much of each other," Bryce said.

Tiffany closed her eyes and said, "Rosemary doesn't think you're worth dumping the other guy for."

"Is that something you saw in a vision?" Bryce asked eagerly. Tiffany had a gift for premonition and had actually foretold his meeting with Rosemary months ago.

"No, you duck-head," Tiffany said, opening her eyes and staring straight at him. "It's obvious."

"Now don't go calling someone a duck-head," Deek badgered.

"But he is a duck-head," she exclaimed. "How can he not see that if Rosemary were really into him, she wouldn't even be thinking about this priest basket?"

Bryce was baffled. He thought for a moment but still couldn't get it. He turned to look at Deek. Deek silently mouthed "bastard."

Great, thought Bryce. *So now Deek has to be my faux profanity translator.*

"Well, what do you recommend I do?" Bryce asked Tiffany.

"I don't know, but stop being such a gosh-darned wimp. That might help," she said.

"Tiffany, we don't speak to our guests that way," Deek explained.

"He asked," she countered in her own defense. "Besides, it's the truth."

Deek sighed. "Honey, the truth is a very valuable thing but we mustn't ever use it as a weapon."

"Oh, you mean like how your sister Cassie said, 'Too bad there were so many opportunities you never had' in that hoity-toity voice of hers?" Tiffany said.

"Cassie was wrong to do that, but we're not going to have an argument about it in front of company," Deek said. Having known Deek many years, Bryce could tell his patience was wearing thin.

"Fine," Tiffany said. "I'll go get dessert." She began clearing her place at the table by piling the plates on top of each other.

"Please don't stack dishes," Deek ordered. "That's revolting."

"Only to people who have so much to eat they can afford to get upset about things like stacking dishes," she said, leaving the room.

Once she was out of earshot, Deek confided in Bryce.

"I lose my temper sometimes, but it's hard to get angry at her when I see what she's been through," he said. "A week after we moved her in here, whenever I went in the pantry or the fridge, I started noticing a lot of the containers only had a tiny bit of food left in the bottom. I asked her why she didn't just finish them up or throw them out, but she kept ignoring me. Finally, she admitted that when she was growing up, they got in trouble for eating things up because that meant their mother would have to buy more, and they never had enough money, so they would always leave some in the bottom to make it look like it wasn't used up. Can you imagine that?"

Bryce was horrified. This woman and her siblings had been punished for *eating*? He was taught never to waste food, of course, but he always knew there would be enough. It was a hard thought to realize Tiffany had been raised knowing full well that there would never be enough. He had to admit it caused him to pity her.

All of a sudden, they heard a crash from the kitchen, followed by Tiffany exclaiming "Melon farmer!"

Deek rushed to the kitchen to see what had happened. Bryce could hear her shouting "I broke the stupid fudging vase!"

"*Vase*," honey, "*vase,*" Deek corrected.

"Fudge you!" screamed Tiffany.

5

Bryce was playing platform tennis with his friend, Topher Van Hees, the following day. Topher was a recovering addict with whom he'd grown up in Ardsley; his therapist had recommended that he get plenty of physical exercise to help with the recovery process, so they regularly got together for a game.

Bryce hated tennis of any kind, despite its popularity with everyone he knew, but platform tennis wasn't so bad. The court reminded him of the plywood stage upon which he'd performed one year at summer camp. He wasn't a good actor. He wasn't a good platform tennis player, either, but it was for a good cause so he didn't mind.

Also, he felt compelled to be kind to Topher because he'd slept with his wife, Stephanie. Stephanie and Bryce had dated in college before he threw her over for the daughter of an Italian diplomat. However, Stephanie had carried a torch for him, and while Topher was in rehab, they'd begun an affair. Bryce had ended it, though, because Stephanie was getting too serious.

Afterwards, she'd moved in with her therapist and divorced Topher. Amazingly, Topher seemed to be handling everything very well for a guy who wasn't too bright. He was doing good work as a consultant to Rosemary at Ben's company, a job Bryce had gotten him.

"I heard from Stephanie yesterday," Topher said as they played. "She's pregnant."

Topher was unable to have children, which was one of the reasons Stephanie left him. Bryce couldn't fathom someone in Topher's position having to hear that bit of news, much less being able to repeat it.

"I'm sorry," he said. "I mean, I'm happy for Stephanie, but I know how that must make you feel."

"Not at all," Topher said. "We've got to live life on life's terms. Stephanie wanted children and now she can have them. Honestly, I'm happy for her."

If Topher had been Catholic, Bryce would've nominated him for sainthood.

Topher added, "But her parents aren't taking it very well."

Bryce could just imagine Mr. and Mrs. Edleman choking on their Martinis at the news that their divorced daughter, who was living with her therapist, was now about to have their first grandchild out of wedlock.

"That must've been an interesting conversation," Bryce said.

"Stephanie told me her mother cried," Topher said. "The 'rents really think she's gone off the rails."

Topher had the annoying habit of using WASP shorthand—saying "'rents" for "parents," and "'za" for "pizza."

"Is there any chance they'll get married?" Bryce asked. It was possible they could avoid a scandal if they wed early enough in the pregnancy.

"No, Ambrose doesn't believe in marriage," Topher said. "Fortunately, though, the baby will have dual citizenship. Ambrose is Canadian."

Like all Americans, Bryce tended to forget that Canada existed. However, being half Canadian could be construed as something of a plus. It would be a good thing for the baby to have multiple citizenships. One could never have enough passports.

"Meanwhile, did I tell you I started dating?" Topher said, smiling.

"No," said Bryce.

"Juliette and I met in rehab and she called me last week. She used to take pills. You're supposed to wait a year before getting involved with someone, but we both promised to take it slowly. You know, starting off as more of a friendship," Topher explained.

"That's great news," Bryce said. "What's she like?"

"She's never been married; her family's from the city. We're a lot alike. Her older sister is a very successful major gifts officer who married the son of a four-star general. They have three perfect sons; the perfect family. She always felt less-than, and pills were a way of escaping, just like they were for me, although she never got into coke like I did," Topher said. "We get along really well."

"That's fantastic," Bryce said. He was happy to think someone out there might care for Topher. He was limited, but he was a good guy who deserved to be loved.

"I even told her I couldn't have children," Topher said, "But she said if we ever got to that point, she would be happy to adopt. Can you imagine that? You know, Bryce, I probably wouldn't be the best dad in the world, but I can tell you I sure would try the hardest."

Suddenly Bryce wanted to cry. He missed the ball as it sailed past him.

"Can we take a quick break?" he asked, heading to the men's locker room.

Something about what Topher had just said had touched him profoundly. He recalled his own father, a distant, nondescript figure who was little more than a placeholder in Bryce's life. His persona was so flimsy that Bryce struggled just to remember him at all, and sometimes practically convinced himself that the man was a figment of the imagination instead of someone who had ever really lived.

Meanwhile Topher, unquestionably the most benighted soul he knew, had already decided to be a conscientious father to an as-yet unadopted child that wouldn't even be his own flesh and blood. It made Bryce feel something he could not name.

Before he knew it, Topher was standing in the locker room with him.

"It's okay, Bryce. It's okay *not* to be okay," was all he said.

Bryce wiped his eyes with his towel. "It's fine, really, I'm just—tired."

"Look, I don't know what you're going through, but I'm your friend. You can tell me anything."

Bryce was suddenly tempted to tell him about the affair he'd had with Stephanie shortly before she left him, but he felt it would be wrong. Topher was still in a vulnerable state of recovery. News like that might push him over the edge. Besides, Bryce rationalized, telling him would only be unburdening his own conscience at the expense of hurting Topher. In the end, he convinced himself that telling Topher about the affair would be dishonorable. He pulled himself together and slapped Topher on the shoulder.

"Thanks," he said, "I appreciate that. Now I'm famished. Let's go get some 'za."

6

Bryce received a strange call from Rosemary that evening. He was sitting by the fire reading Thomas Mann's *The Magic Mountain* when the phone rang. Something about rural Connecticut always made Bryce want to read. He was just getting to the part where the main character was visiting his tubercular cousin in the sanitorium and wishing such places still existed where the unwell could languish.

Rosemary sounded concerned and asked Bryce how he was doing. He told her he was fine.

"What's the matter?" he asked her.

"Nothing," she said. "I just wanted to check up on you. Topher said you were feeling down today."

So that's it, Bryce thought.

He knew Rosemary and Topher were thick as thieves and both had overactive emotional radar. Topher must've been hoping Rosemary could get him to crack. What was he going to tell her? That he was feeling sorry for having a father who alternated between boredom and depression and didn't seem to care about him? That he felt like a cad for sleeping with Stephanie while poor, trusting, stupid Topher was in rehab? He had to come up with something better.

"I'm having a spiritual crisis," he finally announced.

"Okay," said Rosemary in a calm yet attentive voice. "Can you describe it?"

"I'm just questioning my place in the universe and whether or not there's a God, and all that," he said.

Amazingly, Rosemary seemed to believe him. "What you're experiencing is very common," she said. "In fact, most people who reach the point where you are now go on to attain some kind of greater spiritual unfolding, so this is a constructive crisis. Things need to be broken down before they can be built up. Does that make sense?"

It didn't, but Bryce assured her that it did.

"Good," she remarked. "Do you have any idea in what direction you'd like to start traveling to resolve your concerns?"

Bryce barely understood the question, but he knew Rosemary was a spiritual person so he said he'd value her advice.

"Well," she said, "it's always good to begin with whatever spiritual background is already in place in your life. Is there someone at a local Episcopalian church you can talk to?"

Bryce thought a moment. He didn't attend church locally, but there was the church in Tuxedo Park.

"I know a priest at my sister's parish," he said.

"And you feel comfortable talking to this person?" she asked.

Bryce considered the question. Actually, he would feel comfortable talking to Father Jeff.

"Yes," he said.

The rest of the conversation revolved around Rosemary explaining a lot of things that didn't really register with Bryce, such as various paths to the Almighty and spiritual evolution and being a "seeker," but Rosemary was definitely on a roll. It occurred to Bryce that perhaps she was taking such an interest in his crisis because she had a weakness for men undergoing spiritual indecision, like David.

During the conversation, she also told him that David was contemplating leaving the priesthood again, and she wasn't sure how she felt about that.

Bryce said, "If that's what David wants, there's nothing wrong with it, and maybe it would be for the best. The two of you could be together."

"That's just it," Rosemary said. "Regardless of the fact that I have feelings for him, I don't know if he's right for me."

And what about me? Bryce thought, but didn't say. He'd like to meet this David and punch him in the nose for yo-yoing Rosemary around for more than a year, first telling her he had to follow his priestly calling, and then circling back to say his love for her was stronger, only to pull the rug out from under her at the last moment.

One night shortly before Bryce and Rosemary began dating, David had called her from the seminary.

"That's it," he told her. "I'm finished. I'm not meant to be a priest."

Out of love for him and a desire for his happiness, she'd tried to talk him out of it, tried to get him to talk it over with his confessor, but he was adamant. He told her to pack a bag and meet him at Grand Central. He said he'd buy a wedding ring for her on the way down from the seminary and they'd get married and head off somewhere on an impromptu honeymoon.

Four hours later, just as she was about to leave to meet the Acela train from Boston, he called. He told her he couldn't outrun his destiny, so he was staying. Rosemary had lost, yet again, in a tug-of-war with God. Bryce couldn't fathom the level of arrogance it took to do something like that, but then again, David had been a spoiled kid from a rich family in Greenwich, Rhode Island. Rosemary hadn't ever encountered anyone with that level of self-absorption; such utter megalomania was foreign to her, and therefore she couldn't possibly recognize it.

Bryce was from a rich family, though, and he recognized it as soon as she'd begun telling him about David. She explained that she wanted to take things slowly because she was still unsure of her feelings and didn't want to hurt Bryce. She told him all about her whirlwind courtship with David that ended with him breaking her heart. At the time he'd warned her that men like David spend a lifetime breaking things—toys, promises—it was all the same. They were hollow and vain and sought things they could destroy like a tornado seeking low ground.

"I don't know many things, Rosemary, but I know David is going to hurt you again and again," Bryce said.

"You're probably right," Rosemary said, "But my feelings don't work on logic. I need time to get them aligned with my thoughts."

Bryce sighed. The takeaway here was that whatever he was doing, he was still fudging things up. He decided to reference the earlier part of the conversation, saying, "I'll make an appointment with Father Jeff."

Rosemary sounded pleased. "That's a wonderful idea. Even if he can't answer your questions, you'll have taken the first step. As the Buddha said, there are only two mistakes you can make along the road to truth: not going all the way, and not starting."

7

That Friday, Bryce's appointment with Father Jeff wasn't until 4PM, so he realized he could stop at Susan's for tea. He felt crazy going through with the meeting, but he planned to just chat a bit and then be able to report back to Rosemary that he was still in a state of spiritual confusion. He hoped it would move her to spend more time thinking about him than David.

Margaret answered the door. She informed him that Alexandra was still napping when he inquired about seeing the baby. Bryce had forgotten that babies slept all the time.

"How do you like being a godfather?" Margaret asked.

Bryce told her he was enjoying it so far.

"My godfather was a family friend," she explained as she led him to the sitting room where the tea would be served. "Every time he came to the house, he gave me a nickel. You couldn't get me to spend those nickels on anything."

Susan was sitting on the couch and he gave her a quick kiss. She said Patty would be down in a moment, she was just getting dressed.

"So what's going on with this mysterious visit with Father Jeff?" Susan asked.

"Nothing," Bryce answered.

"You're not cracking up, are you?" she asked.

Bryce laughed. "Seriously, is that what you think?"

"I don't have the faintest idea what goes on in that head of yours," Susan said. "Never have."

When she said things like that, she reminded him unpleasantly of Grandfather.

"I'm just going to talk about godfather-type things; you know, my moral responsibilities towards Alexandra and such," he lied.

"He covered all that during our rehearsal," Susan stated. Clearly, she was suspicious.

"Why should you be so upset that I'm meeting with a priest?" he asked.

"Who's upset?" asked Patty, coming into the room.

Susan continued grilling Bryce, saying, "You're meeting with my priest for no apparent reason. What's going on?"

"Oh Susan," said Patty, "That's none of our business."

Susan shot Patty a look. "You're already on thin ice."

Bryce knew better than to get involved in an argument between them. A couple of times in the past he'd stepped in to take Patty's side and Susan had really let him have it.

"You're being very unkind," Patty said to Susan. "I have a right to an opinion about Sandy's care."

"What?" Bryce said, looking puzzled. Patty's comment was so unexpected that he forgot he wasn't supposed to be getting embroiled.

Susan looked towards the kitchen and then leaned over to Bryce and whispered, "We'd planned all along that Margaret would take care of Alexandra. She said she could manage it on top of her other tasks but Patty insists she's overwhelmed and wants to get a nanny."

Just then, Margaret came in with tea. The three of them sat silently while she set down the tray. Bryce felt vaguely guilty that they'd been discussing her behind her back.

After she left and Susan could hear water running in the kitchen, she leaned over to Bryce again. "Margaret would be highly offended if we got a nanny. She's more than capable of taking care of the baby and she wants to. It's a point of pride."

Since they seemed to be including him in the conversation, Bryce felt at liberty to ask a question.

"Did she say—?" he began.

"No," Susan said, "But Patty has taken it upon herself to assume that it's too much for her to handle. And if we get a nanny, Margaret is likely to be so insulted that she'll leave."

"She wouldn't leave," Patty whispered. "She'd probably be relieved."

"I am not going to risk losing a good maid because you want to throw away money on extra help," Susan said, adding, "and that's that," which was how Susan ended arguments when she was trying to be polite.

Just then, the phone rang. A moment later, Margaret appeared at the doorway.

"Call for you, ma'am," she said, looking at Susan. "Your lawyer."

"I'll take it in the study," Susan said.

Susan lumbered down the hall and Margaret went upstairs to check on the baby.

Patty came and sat next to Bryce.

"You know I love Margaret but I'd like Sandy to have a nanny who can speak French, or maybe even an *au pair*. That wouldn't cost as much," she said.

"Good luck," was all Bryce could think of saying. He knew arguing with his sister was futile. He had no idea how Patty put up with her at all, much less decided to raise a child with her. He could see the baby's upbringing as a long string of battles.

After tea, as Bryce was on his way to the church, he couldn't help feeling sad for Susan. She was such a rigid person. Grandfather had molded her carefully during her formative years, including all of his own good qualities and bad. She was excellent at managing finances and running things but she had a hard time understanding others' points of view. Then again, she'd married an artist, so maybe she was vaguely aware that she needed balance in her life.

8

At the church, Bryce was surprised to find Father Jeff in his shirt and collar wearing a tweed sportscoat and jeans. He remembered something about how working people had taken to wearing denim on Fridays and figured maybe it was reflective of that trend.

"Bryce!" Father Jeff said joyously. "Come in." Father Jeff always seemed happy to see everyone.

They walked to the back of the church and behind the altar, where his office was located. Father Jeff indicated a comfy-looking worn leather wingchair.

"Have a seat," he said.

Bryce was about to say something vague about wanting to know more about God, with Father Jeff offering some elaboration—which Bryce was hoping would be enough to kill about 20 minutes—when Father Jeff stopped him.

"Before we begin," the priest said, "I'd like to have a moment of prayer."

Bryce dutifully folded his hands and bowed his head, but the idea of a preliminary prayer took him by surprise. Apparently, this was going to be a more serious meeting than he thought.

"Almighty God," Father Jeff prayed, "Please be present with us as we strive to become better people. Help us to have compassion and understanding, and forgive our failures. Above all, help us to know and accept the magnitude of your love for us. Amen."

"Amen," Bryce said.

"Now then," Father Jeff said, lounging back in his chair and looking at Bryce intently, "What's up?"

Bryce took one look at the young priest's face and he could tell he'd gotten much more than he'd bargained for. Father Jeff's Midwestern bumpkin aura was gone, and he realized, to his dismay, that he was seated across from an astute judge of human behavior. The yokel act was just for the tourists, as it were, and now Bryce had to figure out his opening remarks since "Tell me more about God" clearly wasn't going to wash. This man could practically see into his soul.

"I'm having trouble connecting with God," he said awkwardly. "I thought maybe you could help, but if not, that's fine."

Father Jeff waited a moment before he spoke. He studied Bryce closely.

"Have you ever seen the movie 'How Green Was My Valley'?"

"No," said Bryce.

"Great flick," Father Jeff said. "It's an old 1940s gem about a minister in a small mining village in Wales. At one point, he says something that I think is the definitive statement about what a priest's job is. He says, 'My business is anything that comes between my people and the spirit of God,' so my first question to you is: what is it that's coming between you and the spirit of God? What's interfering with that connection?"

Bryce was in way over his head. He struggled to think of an answer.

"The way I see it," Father Jeff continued, "Our connection to God is like that telephone thing you do when you're a kid with the two tin cans and the string. It's a system that's designed to work, so if it's not working, it's because somebody isn't pulling the string tight enough, and I can assure you, God's always pulling tight enough."

Father Jeff sat up in his chair and went on.

"People come to me and tell me that God's abandoned them, or that God doesn't care about them anymore, but you know what I'm looking at? I'm seeing people who aren't even holding the tin can. The can's on the ground, and meanwhile, they're complaining that God doesn't exist. But sometimes," he said, "I see people who are trying to hold the can and pull it tight. They're doing their best, but the string has knots in it, and that's what's disrupting the connection. Do you think that could be your problem?"

"Yes," Bryce said. "I suppose so." By now, he was just relieved the priest hadn't thrown him out of his office.

"Well then, we need to figure out what kinds of knots you've got. Your Seven Deadlies can do it, or doing any of those things you're not supposed to do according to the Ten Commandments. But believe it or not, those aren't the main culprits," he said.

"They're not?" Bryce said, beginning to become engaged by the metaphor.

"Nope," said Father Jeff, sitting back in his seat again and shaking his head. "I bet the answer will surprise you. Some of the worst knots in that line come from guilt, unworthiness, bitterness, and grief."

"Really?" remarked Bryce. This was becoming interesting.

"People think their problem is that God doesn't love them, when actually, it's mostly their unwillingness to accept the fact that God *does* love them. Pretty ironic, huh?" he asked.

Father Jeff was obviously more than able to carry on a conversation by himself, so he continued.

"If we consider those four states of being—guilt, unworthiness, bitterness, and grief—which one resonates with you the most? Don't answer right away; take a moment to think about it," the priest advised.

Bryce could've told Father Jeff he didn't have to worry about that. Bryce's head was spinning. It would be a miracle if he could come up with even a half-baked answer. Then, for some reason, he remembered the incident earlier in the week with Topher which had brought him close to tears.

"If I had to say," Bryce offered tentatively, "Maybe bitterness and grief."

"Good!" the priest crowed. "Now we're getting somewhere. So maybe bitterness and grief are what's getting between you and the spirit of God. And how do we remove them?"

"I don't know," Bryce said.

"We don't," Father Jeff said. "God does. Trust me, God's much better than we are when it comes to the heavy lifting."

Bryce definitely liked the idea of letting God do the hard work.

"Should I pray for . . . for God to do that?" Bryce asked, hoping to sound like a willing participant.

"Well, yes, but it's not likely to be an instant process. It took a long time to accumulate and it'll take a long time to remove. You didn't hear me say this, but a trained therapist can be really helpful too. Psychological things and spiritual things frequently get tangled up. I'm not a therapist, and you don't have to tell me anything you don't want to, but do you think you could summarize what's going on in 20 words or less?" Father Jeff asked.

"My father—" Bryce began. "He was very distant."

"So part of you is angry and part of you is hurt. Gotcha," Father Jeff noted. "Bitterness and grief. That'll knot up the string every time."

"You make it sound so matter-of-fact," Bryce remarked. He had been pretending to be suffering a spiritual crisis of epic proportions which Father Jeff had quickly reduced to a run-of-the-mill knotty string in his tin-can phone to God. There was something about that which definitely miffed him.

Father Jeff responded, "Actually, this diagnosis is fairly rare because most people don't ever even reach your stage of spiritual introspection, if we're being completely candid here. My job primarily revolves around caring for those members of my congregation whose spiritual evolution is at the very earliest stage, which is most of them."

Bryce didn't know if he could handle a priest who was this blatantly honest.

"When I give a sermon, frankly, I'm hoping enough of it will sink in that they don't kill each other in the parking lot afterwards. Anything beyond that is gravy," Father Jeff added. He went on, saying, "I have a lot of meetings with my congregants, but most of the time it's about them either wanting to whine about their life or tell me how good they are in hopes I'll divulge where to find the secret express elevator to heaven. Give me a good spiritual seeker like you any day."

With that, Father Jeff stood up and offered Bryce his hand.

"Congratulations. I hope that pretty soon you and God will have a lot to talk about," the priest said.

"That's it?" Bryce asked.

"Well, if you insist, I could wave a dead chicken over your head, but I'd have to charge extra," Father Jeff quipped.

That made Bryce think of money. He panicked. Should he ask for a bill? Leave a tip? He was unsure, so he pulled out his wallet and said, "Here, let me give you something for your trouble."

"You know what?" Father Jeff said, "Just drop it in the plate next Sunday. Or not. Makes no difference."

"Okay. I will," Bryce promised, realizing only after he'd said it how ambiguous it sounded.

As Bryce walked to his car, he could've sworn he heard the strains of James Brown singing "Papa's Got a Brand New Bag" coming from Father Jeff's office.

9

On Saturday mornings, Bryce enjoyed having a big breakfast. He was just about to sit down to a plate of fried eggs, ham steak, buttered biscuits, hash browns, and sliced fresh tomatoes seasoned with freshly ground black pepper when a sound outside the cabin startled him. A moment later, he heard a knock at the front door.

Whoever it was must've come on foot, because there was no car. Normally, he would've seen anyone approaching from the front window, but he'd been at the stove cooking breakfast.

He made sure his robe was well tied. He glanced at the mantle clock. It was 11AM. Who would come calling at this hour on a Saturday?

He opened the door to find a couple about his age, clad in flannel.

"Hi there, I'm Norm Fenton and this is my wife, Maddie," the man said, smiling. "We live on the other side of your property," Norm said, gesticulating behind himself.

"What can I do for you?" Bryce asked.

"I hope we're not disturbing you. We came because our dog snuck under the fence last night and we wondered if you've seen her. She's a Black Lab," Norm explained.

"Her name is Suki," Maddie added.

Bryce's first cup of coffee hadn't yet kicked in, but things were starting to fall into place. The Fenton property adjoined his. Old Man Fenton had passed away years ago. Grandfather had liked him. The place then went to his son, who summarily handed it down to his son, whom he realized must be the Norm standing before him. Norm and Maddie must have taken the shortcut over the stone wall at the back end of the property instead of coming up the driveway from the street. Bryce wasn't too happy about that. What if he'd been having sex out in the back woods with someone? Not that he ever did such a thing, but he surely wouldn't be expecting neighbors to come walking up on him if he did.

He also remembered Grandfather having said something about the couple being overly friendly, and that their dog was constantly escaping. After a few times, he'd put a stop to it by threatening to call the authorities if they didn't confine the animal properly, and he didn't have any trouble after that, but the Fentons had probably heard of Grandfather's death and waited to see who would take over the cabin. That's probably why Bryce hadn't heard from them until now.

He realized, with no small chagrin, that right here, right now, before even partaking of his breakfast, he was going to have to either show himself to be a kinder, gentler person than Grandfather on the crucial matter of establishing neighborly relations, or reiterate the hardline position Grandfather had taken, in hopes of stemming any future unpleasantness, which might possibly include the Fentons hopping the fence whenever they had nothing better to do, which he guessed would be often. Also, that he was their age probably encouraged them to think they could make free with him in ways they might not have attempted with Grandfather, crotchety old bird that he had been.

Bryce was highly displeased. Having to make decisions tantamount to foreign policy (on the personal level) on the spot and on an empty stomach was intolerable, but he would have to do his best.

"I'm afraid I haven't seen Suki, but I'll keep an eye out for her," he started. Before he could continue, Maddie responded effusively.

"Oh, thank you so much. She's such a silly girl. She usually comes back in a day or two but we worry about her. She's a great dog. Are you a dog person? I'm sorry, I didn't get your name," she said.

"Bryce," he said, hoping to get out of the exchange by offering as little personal information as possible. He was scrupulous about guarding his privacy and he had a feeling Norm and Maddie were going to put him in the uncomfortable position of having to refuse their attempts to get to know him.

"Good to know you, Bryce," Norm said, offering his hand. "You know, we have a fire pit at our place and about once a month we get together with a couple of friends; you know, have a few beers and throw something on the grill. We'd love for you to join us."

Occasionally Bryce heard hooting and hollering from that part of the woods of an otherwise peaceful weekend evening. Now he knew why.

Bryce was about to respond when Maddie took a piece of paper out of her pocket and handed it to him.

"Here's our phone number, in case you see Suki," she said.

Then, to Bryce's horror, she pulled a cellphone out of the same pocket.

"And what's your number?" she asked.

Bryce's future happiness and sanity now rested on one of only two choices. He could give Maddie his number and hope they would not abuse it. In his experience of human nature dealing with people not of his background, this would invariably lead to disaster. The other option was to give them a wrong number.

He rattled off his phone number but transposed the last two digits. He could always later claim to have dyslexia.

"So, what do you like to do, Bryce? Are you a hiker?" Norm asked. "Lots of great trails around here. Maddie and I hike all the time."

Bryce sensed that this was his opening. It was the only angle from which he might get a clear shot, so he figured he'd better take it.

"Actually, I'm quite busy. I do appreciate your offer to come over, but I'm usually not up for that kind of thing. And speaking of, I hate to ask this, but I wonder if you wouldn't mind coming up the front drive if you ever have to come here again. I really don't like people wandering around the back woods, if you know what I mean," he said, hoping he'd struck the perfect balance between courteousness and firmness.

One look at their faces, however, and Bryce saw that he had not.

"Look, Bryce, we were just trying to be neighborly," Norm said.

Maddie looked crestfallen.

"If you'd lost your dog, we'd gladly help you," she said.

Bryce felt cornered.

"I don't mind about the dog. I mean, I'll keep an eye out for her. I'll call if I see her. I just don't care to have strangers roaming around my property. I don't go vaulting over into your yard," he said, laughing lightly, hoping that would cut the tension that was developing.

Maddie said, "But we *invited* you into our yard. We were hoping to be friends."

Bryce took a deep breath. "I apologize if I've given you the impression that I'm unfriendly. I'm simply a very busy, private person and while I want to have a good relationship with you, I don't foresee spending a lot of time at your place. I'd also appreciate it if you'd refrain from coming into my woods. That's all."

"Okay, fine," Norm said, backing away. Maddie followed. "If you happen to see Suki, give us a call if it's not too much trouble. Thanks. Sorry to have intruded."

Bryce heard them muttering to each other as they walked along the driveway to the street.

"I hope she turns up soon," he called out after them.

After he shut the door, he realized that not only had he created an adversarial relationship and offended their hospitality, but he'd almost certainly exposed himself as a subject of local gossip. People in small towns always talked, and particularly about rich families like his. Grandfather had created a good reputation as a fair man who liked his privacy. Somehow, he'd pulled off simply being an aloof gentleman, whereas Bryce feared he was going to be characterized as a lofty prick. He could just imagine Norm and Maddie sitting around their next fire pit gathering with friends, remarking, "We invited the guy next door, but he didn't want anything to do with us. Practically threw us off his front steps. Can you believe it?" Somewhere in there, his being a dog-hater would probably get mentioned. That would really be the end of him. You could be a lot of things and some people might still like and defend you, but everyone hated a dog-hater.

Now Bryce was half hoping that Suki would show up at his place so he could return her to the Fentons and let them see that he did, in fact, like dogs very much.

Still, on balance, he thought that what he did was probably preferrable to what would've happened had he freely given information to the couple. The phone would be ringing off the hook. He'd emerge from the cabin to find them (and possibly their friends) picking wildflowers in his yard or gathering acorns or whatever they did. It was all about setting boundaries, he concluded, and he'd unquestionably done that. Now he had to let the chips fall where they may.

His breakfast was cold and he wished he'd never answered the door. Maybe it was time for a butler.

10

On Monday, he met Rosemary in the city to go over some loose ends about a project he'd worked on months before, but she was particularly focused on his "spiritual journey," as she called it. She wanted to know all about his meeting with Father Jeff.

Bryce told her they'd discussed what might be interfering with his connection to God. Rosemary seemed impressed. He was delighted thinking this had possibly turned the tide of her affections from the wavering would-be priest to him. He thought of asking her to go away on a trip with him. However, she returned to the spiritual matter. With no small annoyance, Bryce was beginning to realize this spiritual evolution thing was her Holy Grail. She wouldn't rest until he was sitting on a mountaintop in a loincloth.

"What's your next step?" she asked.

Bryce was really going to have to come up with something spectacular. A pilgrimage to Mecca? Crawling for miles on his knees to the Shrine of St. James in Santiago de Compostela?

"That's what I was hoping I could discuss with you," he said.

Almost immediately, Rosemary chimed in with, "It's important not to feel daunted early on in the process. It's like climbing a mountain," she explained. "Don't look up. Just keep climbing and you'll get there."

"Okay," Bryce nodded in agreement. "I'll keep on."

"Absolutely," Rosemary said. Bryce could tell she was really eating this up.

"I'm just confused about where to turn next because I'm still so unsure of where I'm going," he said. "How does one find the way?"

Rosemary launched into a short lecture about the inner spiritual compass, and the principle of following things that resonate within. She expounded upon the concept that enlightenment occurs like the coming of high tide, steadily making progress inward but with frequent (though gradually less and less severe) setbacks along the way.

For something that was utterly intangible, Bryce marveled that people had so damn much to say about spirituality.

He was getting bored and hoped she'd come up with some next step for him to take so he could feel her out about possibly visiting him that weekend. They could have dinner at the Red Lion Inn in Stockbridge, Massachusetts. It had one of the few great old New England restaurants.

"I really believe you'd benefit from a retreat," Rosemary was saying.

"I live in a remote cabin in the woods," Bryce said.

Rosemary laughed. "No," she said, "You need guidance, training, and the camaraderie of other spiritual seekers."

"Kind of like *The Canterbury Tales*?" he asked.

"Well, not exactly, but kind of," she said. "There are several good men's ones and I've heard great things about Native American ones. Do you have a preference?"

Bryce had to admit that the thought of a Native American retreat piqued his interest. He couldn't imagine what they'd do, but he was game. Besides, Rosemary seemed the most excited by that option, so she'd probably give him a lot of brownie points for trying it.

"Native American," he said.

"Wonderful! I'll make the arrangements and get back to you, okay?" she asked.

"Sounds great," he said. "Actually, now that that's settled, I wanted to see if you'd be up for a visit to the cabin this weekend. We could have dinner in Stockbridge."

Rosemary was taking a swallow of her coffee and she almost choked because Bryce's question made her laugh.

"Oddly enough, I'm going to a women's retreat this weekend," she said.

"Oh," Bryce said. "That's terrific," adding, "You'll have to tell me all about it."

11

The phone rang later that day as Bryce was seeing off the cleaning lady. Since he was a bachelor and the cabin was small, he didn't bother with full-time staff, but he did keep Mrs. Johnson on for cleaning twice a week, Monday and Friday. She'd worked for Grandfather for ages and did an excellent job. Also, she was nearsighted and hard of hearing, so she wasn't apt to be nosy about his business while she was around.

Growing up in Ardsley, his family's maid had been Delia. She was live-in and cooked very nicely. She was also pretty good with him and Susan. The only problem was that she was a bit of a snoop. His mother had warned them not to discuss anything personal—particularly about financial things—while she was around, and if they slipped while she was within earshot, she'd remind them "*Pas devant les domestiques*," French for "Not in front of the servants." Delia didn't speak French, so she'd take it for a foreign phrase or motto, which it was, but she wouldn't realize it had been said about her.

After he closed the door behind Mrs. Johnson, he answered the phone. It was Deek. He didn't sound too good.

Deek explained that he and Tiffany had attended the Habitat for Humanity gala that weekend.

"How did Tiffany do?" Bryce asked anxiously. He knew this gala was going to be the first big test of her ability to carry herself in polite society.

“Not great but not awful, I suppose,” Deek said.

Just then, Bryce heard a commotion in the background and Deek saying, “Well you’re back early, Honey.” He guessed Deek thought he’d be alone for a while.

He could hear Tiffany asking who was on the phone. Evidently, Deek hadn’t yet taught her about respecting the privacy of others. When Deek told her that it was Bryce, he could hear Tiffany insisting, “Put me on speaker! Put me on speaker!”

What is it with the lower classes and speakerphone? he thought. They were simply drawn to chaos like moths to a flame. Bryce heard the sound of a click.

“Bryce,” Tiffany shouted.

“Hello Tiffany. How are you?” Bryce asked.

“I gotta ask you about something,” she said.

Bryce was surprised, but said, “Okay. Sure. What is it?”

“Would you pay four-hundred dollars for a jar of cookies?”

Bryce surmised this had something to do with items for sale at the gala.

“Would you?” she demanded.

“That depends,” he said. “If you’re talking about a box of cookies in the grocery store, no, but if this is something to do with the gala—”

Tiffany cut him off.

“You people are fudged in the head! All of you!” she exclaimed. “You wouldn’t catch me paying four-hundred dollars for a jar of chocolate-chip cookies unless they were laced with coke!”

“Sweetheart, I think you’re missing the point,” Deek said. Then he addressed Bryce, explaining, “It was part of the auction.”

“Tiffany,” Bryce said, “You’re absolutely right—the cookies aren’t worth four-hundred dollars, but the idea of the gala, as I’m sure Deek told you, is to raise money. So people donate things, like gift certificates or works of art or cookies, and people bid a lot of money for them, often much more than they’re worth. It’s for charity.”

“I don’t get it,” she said. “If someone wants to give money to Habitat for Humanity, why don’t they just give it to them? Why do they have to make a big show in front of everybody?”

Bryce realized there were a lot of things he could tell her, all of which fell under the heading “How Rich People Think,” but ultimately, he knew Tiffany would never understand.

Deek said, “Before we got there, I told Tiffany she could have a thousand dollars to spend however she wanted. She could bid on anything, or buy anything, and all the money would go to charity, but tell Bryce where the money is," said Deek, turning the conversation back over to Tiffany.

"In my purse," she said flatly. "I'm my favorite charity."

Bryce had an idea. "You know, Tiffany, charities don't just need money, they need time. Have you thought about getting involved with Habitat?"

"Funny you should mention that," said Deek. "We ran into an acquaintance of mine at the gala who invited Tiffany to join the Board of Directors, but she wasn't very receptive."

"I don't want to sit on no board," she said.

"*Any* board," Deek corrected.

Bryce said, "I meant volunteering to work on the houses."

"I can't build a house, you duck-head," Tiffany said.

"No, you don't have to. They help you and teach you how to do things," Bryce said. A friend of his had worked on a Habitat project once and liked it.

Bryce heard a commotion on the other end and then a click, which meant he was back to having a private conversation with Deek, or so he thought until he realized the line had gone dead. He shrugged and hung up the phone. Tiffany was probably having some kind of tantrum that caused Deek to abandon the call. Bryce wondered if Deek were changing Tiffany or if it were actually the other way around.

Moments later, while he was getting a glass of tomato juice, the phone rang again. This time it was Rosemary. She sounded exuberant.

"I've got you signed up for a one-day spiritual renewal. It's in Massachusetts. I think it'll be perfect for you."

Bryce was glad it was only one day. That sounded manageable.

Rosemary explained it would be on Saturday.

"And I have a surprise for you," she said happily. "Topher is going with you."

Ordinarily he would've been glad of the company during something that had the potential to be stultifyingly boring, but then he realized Topher would probably take the opportunity to discuss all kinds of spiritual things, since he'd learned all about that stuff in recovery. Why was it that people who saw the light felt so compelled to share it with everyone around them? Bryce was perfectly content being a spiritual troglodyte.

"Well then, I guess you and I will both be doing our spiritual fine-tuning this weekend," he said, not sure exactly what to call it.

"Oh, that's the funny thing," Rosemary said. "David just called and wants to meet with me. The only day he can make it is Saturday, so I cancelled my retreat."

David was training to be a priest. Rosemary had made it sound like he had the schedule of a Joint Chief of Staff. How could his calendar possibly be so packed? And why was she unwilling to cancel her retreat to be with him, yet she dropped everything when David called?

"Why does he want to meet with you?" Bryce asked.

"It's not what you think," she said. "He needs a friend's advice."

"And I can see why villains like him don't have many friends," Bryce said.

"Bryce, that's not very nice," Rosemary said. "This is why I can't talk to you. David never speaks that way."

"No," Bryce said. "He just treats your heart like a piñata."

"Nothing he does is intentional," Rosemary said. "He's just being as honest with me as he can, and right now, he needs my help."

Bryce knew it was no use arguing with Rosemary when she was entrenched in her defense of David. He was also having flashbacks to conversations with Leslie, his late friend, when she would defend the man who was misusing her. No amount of evidence proving he was a complete scoundrel would convince her. However, when it did finally register, she swallowed a bottle of pills, so maybe it was better that Rosemary remain in a state of willful ignorance. At least she was alive.

At that point, Rosemary said she had to go; she was late for a meeting, so they said goodbye.

Bryce was just about to run an errand in town when the phone rang yet again. Sometimes it just felt like Grand Central around his place. This was one of those days.

"Hello?" he said.

"Bryce, this is Cricket," said a voice on the other end, sending Bryce into a state of distress.

"How did you get my number?" he asked.

"Topher Van Hees gave it to me," she said.

It figured that Topher wouldn't have a clue that nobody in their right mind wanted to talk to Cricket, but Topher wasn't the sharpest guy. Bryce made a mental note to kill him Saturday on the way to the spiritual renewal retreat.

One of the blessings of having moved to the cabin was being able to not give his landline number to certain people, Cricket being one of them. He'd all but convinced himself he'd never have to speak to her again, save for perhaps a chance meeting at a social event, but their social circles didn't overlap too much these days.

She was calling to continue a conversation they'd had a year ago in which she was trying to guilt him into paying for some kind of dues or upkeep or something-or-other for a club to which he and his family had belonged for generations. Cricket was the consummate committee-woman, always making calls and following up with people and generally being a colossal nuisance. They'd gone to school together and Bryce remembered she was always the girl who tattled on everyone.

He was doing his best to block out whatever she was saying, but he caught fragments of it, something about "the good of the institution," and "bettering our world," and "misplaced priorities." By the time she got to "letting standards slip," he decided to join the conversation.

"I couldn't agree more," he told her. "We are so very lucky to have you at the helm, Cricket."

"Don't patronize me," she said. "You know I mean you."

"I'm afraid that can't be," he said. "My financial commitments have been updated entirely because of and due to the fault of those who have let standards slip," hoping the excuse would be unintelligible enough to make her think he'd said something profound.

"In that case, you need to re-update your financial commitments and include us. And don't think that because Nathalie and your sister back you up that the rest of us don't know what kind of person you really are."

Bryce was suddenly angry. Cricket had gone too far.

Cricket continued. "And especially don't think that they'll be well thought of for much longer, between Nathalie marrying that Chinese mafioso and Susan being—"

Bryce had always been able to contain his temper, but the torrent of fury rising within him was unstoppable.

His condemnation came out in an unbroken stream. He said, "You petty, pathetic, little nobody. Don't you dare say a word about Nathalie or my sister. A streetwalker has more class than you. And I don't know where you got it into that sand-filled head of yours that you have some kind of power over me, because I can have you ousted with one phone call, and you know it."

Rather than being cowed, Cricket rose even more defiantly.

"I'd like to see you try it," she said. "Then you'll find out what everyone really thinks of the Parnells."

"Get back on your broomstick," he said, hanging up. He couldn't believe her audacity. Old Money people like her disgusted him. They lived in a tiny world of their own importance, propped up by the approbation of others who were just as smug. Their pride was wholly unfounded, and often, they looked down contemptuously on those who were infinitely further above them, as in this case. Bryce's family could buy and sell Cricket's twenty times over, probably more. They were nothing better than peddlers, them and their tatty department store chain. How dare she criticize Susan and Nathalie?

12

Bryce had been so steamed he'd gone out for a walk to burn off some of his agitation, but it didn't work. He decided maybe doing something energetic, like chopping firewood, might be a good activity. He rummaged around in the shed and found an axe. The woodcutting stump was near the house and he found some logs lying around. He placed one on the stump and tried chopping it, but it kept falling over. When it did finally connect with the axe, the axe glanced off the log but it still had so much momentum, it swung down, nearly chopping off the side of Bryce's ankle.

There was no pain, but he felt a funny stinging sensation and saw a lot of blood. Bryce realized his injury was probably serious. He should get into the house and try to wrap it with something, he thought.

Then he heard the rustle of leaves and a huff-puffing sound. Turning to look, he saw a pudgy Black Labrador trotting towards him. Her tail was wagging.

How can a dog that keeps running away be so fat? he wondered.

Now he'd have to call Norm and Maddie besides figuring out how to tend his wound. At least he didn't have to worry about the dog running off again. She seemed preoccupied with bumping her nose into him.

He limped into the house. The dog seemed reluctant to follow him inside. Bryce couldn't remember her name. He knew it was something short, ending with an "ee" sound.

"Come on, Polly."

No response.

"Inside, Sherry."

Bryce was afraid he'd start to bleed all over the rug if he kept standing there guessing her name, so he just went to the phone and kept an eye on her through the open door. When he glanced towards the kitchen, he got the idea of offering her a treat. That would probably get her in.

In the kitchen, the first thing his eyes fell on was a box of Hershey bars. Bryce favored fine Belgian chocolates, but he associated Hershey bars with his childhood because grandfather always bought them in the wintertime when they were visiting the cabin. He said they helped keep you warm. He grabbed a bar and ripped the covering open with one hand. Leaning the corner of the candy bar on the counter, he broke off a square and held it out.

"Here doggie, here's a treat for you," he called.

She came running and eagerly devoured the bit of candy. She looked at him and licked her lips. He gave her another couple of squares, then walked over and closed the front door, covering his wound with some paper towels from the kitchen before he did. Then he sat down next to the phone, where he'd left the piece of paper with the Fenton's phone number.

"Hello?" Norm answered.

"Hi, Norm," Bryce said. "This is Bryce from next door."

"Hi," Norm said.

"Listen, I've got your dog here. She just came over while I was out cutting some wood, so I brought her into the house. I'd walk her over to your place, but I hurt myself, so maybe if you could come and get her—"

"With the axe?" Norm asked.

"Yes, on my ankle," Bryce said.

"Is it bleeding a lot?" he asked.

"Well," said Bryce, looking down and seeing that the paper towels were quickly becoming saturated, "Yes, it is."

"Is your front door unlocked?" Norm asked.

"Yes," Bryce answered.

"Good. You stay there, we'll be right over," Norm said, and hung up.

Bryce started feeling a little woozy but he attributed it to the stress of almost amputating his own foot. Besides, he wasn't too crazy about the sight of blood, especially when it was his.

The dog—whatever her name was—was still standing in the kitchen, staring over at him. He limped back to the counter and grabbed the Hershey bar, returning to his seat with it. The dog followed.

"You like this, huh?" he said, breaking the chocolate into squares which he fed her one at a time. She seemed very happy. Bryce was glad. At least someone was having a good time.

Within minutes, the door flung open and Norm and Maddie rushed to Bryce's side.

"Come on, buddy, we're taking you to the hospital," Norm said. "Maddie already called it in."

The two of them got on either side of Bryce and helped him into Norm's old red truck, which was parked in front of the house. Norm drove and Maddie sat on the passenger side, with Bryce in the middle. He felt odd to be sitting so close to them considering their first conversation had left them feeling upset.

The dog was in the back of the truck, but they'd left the sliding back window open a little so she could see into the cab.

"How's my silly girl?" Maddie said affectionately.

The dog poked her nose through the opening in the window and into Bryce's head. He could feel her slobbering on his hair.

"How's my silly Suki?" Maddie repeated.

Suki. That was it, thought Bryce.

"Thank you so much for finding her," Maddie said. "Actually, she came back two days ago, but then she ran away again this morning."

"How does she get out?" Bryce asked.

"We don't know," Maddie said.

The dog's been escaping for years and they have no idea how? Bryce thought. *She's smarter than they are.*

Bryce cleared his throat. "I feel pretty embarrassed about this," he said, indicating his foot. "I hadn't meant for you to have to—"

"Say no more," Norm said. "This is what neighbors do. We help each other."

When they arrived at the emergency room, they were whisked right in to see a doctor thanks to Maddie's having notified them in advance. Bryce had to admit they were definitely good people to know in a crisis. He'd have to do something special to show his appreciation when this was all over. Maybe he'd even go to one of their fire pit hootenannies.

In the examination area, the doctor took one look at him and proclaimed "So this is our log-splitter!"

Another doctor, hearing him, poked his head around the screen, grinning.

"Congratulations! You're the first one this season!" he announced.

Bryce was indignant.

"We see a lot of this in here this time of year," the doctor said, taking a look at his ankle. "In fact, my diagnosis is that you've definitely had an axe-ident."

Everyone's a comedian, thought Bryce peevishly.

"Can you tell if I'm going to lose my foot or not?" Bryce asked.

The doctor looked at him over the top of his glasses. "You'll go home with both feet. You just skinned yourself pretty good. Nothing a clean dressing can't heal."

As he cleaned the wound, the doctor said, "I'm not at liberty to name names, but just about this time last year, we had an Academy Award-winning actor in here with almost the exact same injury. Owns a farm over in Kent. He was splitting logs too. So you see? You're in good company."

Bryce failed to see how being compared to a clumsy actor was supposed to make him feel better.

After bandaging him, the doctor gave him some kind of shot.

"I'm scheduled to go to a Native American workshop this weekend," Bryce said. "Should I still attend?"

"Yes. In fact, I encourage you to go, especially if they're going to teach you how to cut wood," the doctor said.

After that, Bryce went to the clerk's desk and took care of the paperwork, then he and Norm and Maddie walked to the parking lot, where Suki was waiting for them in the truck.

However, when Maddie peered over the side into the back, she emitted a little scream. Bryce and Norm swung around and looked, whereupon they saw Suki lying down in the truck bed. She was having tremors and there was vomit everywhere.

"Suki!" Maddie cried. She leapt into the back of the truck and cradled the dog in her lap.

"Bryce, get in," Norm ordered. They jumped into the vehicle and Norm sped off for the emergency veterinary hospital.

"How is she?" Norm called out through the sliding window a few minutes later.

"She's breathing," Maddie shouted, "But she's still having tremors."

It was twilight when they reached the veterinary hospital. Norm slammed the truck into park and they raced the dog in. Norm carried Suki in his arms. Her head hung limply over his elbow. Bryce thought she was dead.

Norm placed her on the table. She was twitching as the vet began to examine her.

"Has she had seizures before?" she asked.

"No," Maddie answered. "She's never had them."

"Any history of serious illness?"

"None at all," Maddie said. "She's always been healthy."

Suddenly, Suki turned her head and made a choking sound. Some frothy vomit issued forth onto the examination table.

The vet leaned down and looked closely at the vomit. She sniffed.

"She's been eating chocolate," the vet said.

"Chocolate?!" Norm and Maddie shrieked in unison.

"Where would she get ahold of chocolate?" Maddie asked, horrified.

"We've got to induce vomiting immediately to get as much of it out of her stomach as we can. Then I'll give her activated charcoal to draw the toxicity out of her bloodstream. I'll probably want to keep her overnight just to be safe," the vet said, gesturing to her assistant to carry Suki into the back. The last thing Bryce saw as she rounded the doorway was Suki's tongue lolling out of the side of her mouth.

"Is she going to be okay?" Norm asked.

"She must've ingested it within the last two hours or so, I'd say, so I don't think it's been in her system long enough to be fatal, but she's going to be a very sick girl," the doctor said gravely, heading into the back.

She turned and looked over her shoulder, repeating "A *very* sick girl."

Norm, Maddie, and Bryce went out to the waiting room. Bryce was so overwhelmed with what a bad thing he had done, he almost stopped breathing. He could feel his face burning.

"Where do you think she got the chocolate?" Maddie asked Norm.

"Maybe she got into someone's trash, but she's never been a trash-digger," Norm theorized.

"Maybe she just found it, you know, in the woods," Bryce offered nervously. His hands were starting to shake.

"In the woods?" Norm asked. "Nobody leaves candy lying around in the woods."

"Trick-or-treaters," Bryce suggested.

"Halloween isn't until next week," Maddie said.

Bryce swallowed hard. "It could be that she reacted badly to that snack I gave her."

"What snack?" Maddie asked.

"Just a little bit of candy. So she would come into the house and not run away. I think it was chocolate," he said. "I was pretty dazed from the accident at that point, so there's no telling."

Norm confronted him. "Wait a minute, you think you might have fed her some chocolate? How much?"

"I don't exactly know because it was a little bit at a time," Bryce explained, "to keep her from panicking because she wasn't with you. I figured she'd be frightened in a stranger's house—"

"What kind of chocolate?" Maddie asked, with growing curiosity. "Like M&Ms?"

"It was a Hershey bar, I think," Bryce said. "But only a little bit at a time, like I said. I was dazed."

"You fed our dog a Hershey bar?" Norm shouted. He was outraged.

"You poisoned Suki!" Maddie screamed. The attendants at the desk got up and Bryce could see they were coming over.

"No, no, it was nothing like that," Bryce protested.

"Why would you poison her?" Maddie cried, tears suddenly streaming down her cheeks. Norm put his arm around her and glared at Bryce. Maddie began to sob, punctuated by heaving gasps for breath.

"What happened?" one of the attendants asked.

"This man poisoned our dog," Norm said, accusing Bryce.

"It was an accident. I didn't know until just now that chocolate isn't good for dogs," Bryce pleaded.

"*Isn't good*?" the attendant repeated angrily. "It's toxic. Highly toxic. Dogs can even die from chocolate poisoning. It's no laughing matter."

Bryce wondered why she'd said that. He wasn't laughing. In fact, he felt like throwing up.

"Didn't you ever have a dog?" Maddie asked, still sobbing, yet trying to comprehend the depths of Bryce's monstrosity.

"Yes, we owned a couple of them growing up, but I didn't—" he began.

"When they taught you how to feed them, didn't they tell you about never giving them chocolate?" asked the other attendant.

"We didn't feed them. Delia, our maid, took care of that," Bryce said.

What followed next was highly unpleasant. The attendants went away shaking their heads. Bryce attempted unsuccessfully to apologize to Norm and Maddie, only to be told that he'd do well to call a cab to take him home, as they were staying to wait for updates on Suki's condition.

He thought of offering to buy them another dog if Suki died, but he had a feeling they might take it the wrong way. Their emotions were still raw.

Having to sit in the waiting room until the cab came, with the attendants refusing to even make eye contact with him, and seeing Maddie weep, while Norm repeated "Our poor Suki," over and over, was about the closest thing to hell Bryce had ever encountered on earth.

13

Before he knew it, it was Saturday and Bryce was standing at the sign-in table of the spiritual renewal workshop with Topher at a community center in Central Massachusetts. A tall Native American man greeted him warmly. His name was Don. Bryce was disappointed. He was expecting something more exotic. After exchanging pleasantries with the men, Don handed each of them a schedule and told them to help themselves to coffee until the first session started.

As Bryce sipped the coffee, which was horrible, he looked over the list.

The workshop was to begin with a group meditation, followed by some kind of esoteric outdoor activity that Bryce couldn't quite decipher from the explanation provided, and then lunch. Afterwards, there would be a lecture by a shaman from Arizona, an opportunity to discover his spirit-animal, and then dinner, after which there would be a drum circle. Bryce had a vague notion of what the latter was.

"The drum circle is the best part," said Topher, smiling broadly. "I mean, it's all good, but the drum circle is really amazing."

Bryce looked around. Most of the men in attendance were what Bryce would describe as solidly middle-class, although there were a few biker-types, as well as a few pretentious executive-looking characters who were probably trying to appear enlightened. He could see them at a cocktail party dropping phrases like, "Reminds me of something I experienced at a drum circle last weekend," or "That's something I was discussing with a tribal spiritual leader recently."

Don called the men to order and everyone sat down. He introduced the two co-directors of the workshop, whom he said belonged to his tribe. One was named Harvey and the other was Little Bear.

Bryce found the meditation that followed to be very relaxing. If anything, he realized these spiritual events lowered his stress level.

The outdoor activity was something to do with facing different directions. Topher had trouble identifying which way was east until Bryce reminded him it was the direction from whence the sun was rising. He'd always had trouble with basics like that, even as a kid, Bryce reflected. However, he seemed to get a lot more out of the exercise than Bryce did.

During lunch, the men were encouraged to socialize. They were handed paper bags containing peanut butter sandwiches, carrot sticks, and potato chips. Somehow, Bryce had a different idea about what they might be eating, but when he said so to Topher, Topher assured him that the dinner would be fantastic.

Bryce wanted to sit indoors at a table, preferably with the snobbish executive-looking types, even though he knew he'd hate them, but Topher motioned for him to come outside, where he summarily plunked himself down on the grass next to two hippy-looking men about their age.

Bryce reluctantly joined him.

"I'm Darryl," said one of the men, who had a blonde beard and moustache. "This is Aster," he added, indicating the other man, who was brown-haired and very good-looking.

Topher introduced himself and Bryce.

"Hey Bryce," said Aster. "You have a very good aura. Doesn't he?" he said, turning to Darryl.

Darryl looked at Bryce and smiled. "Yeah, he does. He definitely does."

"Is this your first time at a spirituality workshop?" Aster asked.

Bryce wondered if it showed. "Yes, as a matter of fact."

"Cool. That's really great," Aster commented.

Bryce could feel his brain suffocating. If the conversation didn't pick up quickly, he would lapse into a coma.

"Have you heard Len Fernando speak before?" Darryl asked, referring to the shaman giving the afternoon lecture.

"No," said Topher, struggling with his mouth full of peanut butter, "But I know a guy who studied under him in Chandler two years ago. He said he's amazing."

Bryce felt somewhat excluded. He didn't have anything otherworldly to offer.

"Bryce has just started on his inner journey," Topher explained, hoping to draw him into the conversation.

“That’s great, man,” Darryl said.

Aster turned towards Bryce and, taking the sandwich from Bryce’s hand, he put it down on top of the paper bag. He took both of Bryce’s hands in his and sat with his eyes closed for a moment. Bryce was too shocked to react. When Aster let go of his hands, he told Bryce that he’d given him a surge of heart-energy to bless him on his way.

Bryce wasn’t sure how to react.

“Thanks,” he said. Then he mused, “Aster—that’s a name you don’t hear very often.”

“It was given to me,” Aster said.

“You mean by your parents,” Bryce clarified.

“No,” Aster said flatly. “By a being from the Pleiades.” He sounded serious.

“The constellation the Pleiades?” Bryce asked.

“Yes,” Aster explained. “Some people might not understand, but my name was a gift.”

Bryce decided to dive right in. “How was it given to you?”

Aster looked at him as if he were stupid. “I felt a presence and a voice said ‘Your name is Aster.’”

Ask a silly question, thought Bryce.

“That’s really special,” Topher commented. “There’s so much that people don’t know.”

“Well,” explained Aster, “It’s partly ignorance and it’s partly people who can’t access their own feelings, and this spiritual enslavement is perpetuated by people who make feeling wrong. We’re feeling beings. We feel. And there’s nothing more beautiful in the world than being able to feel openly and honestly. Frankly, that scares the living shit out of most people.”

“See those guys over there?” Darryl said, indicating the executive-looking types who’d come outside for a bit of fresh air.

“Aren’t they too much?” Aster said. Bryce imagined the executives would say the same about him and Darryl, with their woven leather necklaces and Celtic tattoos and wiggy-looking footwear.

Aster laughed disdainfully. “Those guys—if anyone truly looked deeply into their eyes and connected with their soul, I think their heads would explode.”

Bryce had to agree with him there.

“It’s because they don’t know love,” Aster said.

Bryce had a sudden mischievous inspiration. “Funny you should say that, Aster, because they spoke so well of you.”

Aster was astonished. “What do you mean?”

“When I was in the men’s room before we got our lunch, I couldn’t help overhearing them talk about you. They said they wished they could be like you,” Bryce said.

“They said that?” he asked.

“Oh, they said a lot of other things, but I didn’t catch it all and then I left, but I do remember a few comments,” Bryce said.

Aster was all ears. Clearly the guy was an egomaniac. “What were the comments?”

“Well, I remember them particularly because they were so effusive,” Bryce said.

“Wait a minute,” Aster said, “How could they have so much to say about me? I haven’t even spoken to them.”

“Are you kidding?” Bryce asked. “They were standing near you at one point this morning and I guess they either overheard you talking or sensed your aura—I’m not sure—but you made quite an impression. For instance, they said your unaffected openness was the most refreshing thing they’d ever seen.”

“Aster is the most open guy I know,” Darryl concurred.

“I have to be,” Aster asserted. “I share my heart. That’s part of my purpose.”

Aster was obviously dying to hear more about himself, but Bryce wrapped up the conversation with, “I shouldn’t say anything else. I’ve probably already embarrassed you by telling you this much. Anyone can see you’re too humble a person to have any interest in whatever praise others have for you. I’m sorry I mentioned it. Please, let’s talk about something else.”

The conversation then turned to favored fragrances of incense, with Darryl asserting that nag champa was superior, and Topher heartily agreeing with him, but Aster was visibly distracted. It was all Bryce could do to contain his mirth.

Following lunch, there was a lot of excitement as everyone took their seats in the main hall. Bryce always enjoyed a good lecture, so he was actually looking forward to hearing the speaker. Don introduced Len Fernando and said a little about what it meant to be a shaman as a healer and community figure and bridge between the physical and spiritual worlds. Bryce gathered it was something like being a town manager, but with the ability to perform rituals.

Len Fernando sat so still during Don’s introduction and even afterwards that Bryce wondered if something were wrong with him. He looked about seventy. Bryce squinted, hoping to see if the man was blinking or not.

After a long silence, Len Fernando spoke, very clearly and very simply, about spiritual matters. His voice wasn’t animated, but it was interesting in a way Bryce couldn’t define. Everything he said made sense, even though he was talking about ephemeral things like the “oneness of everything” and other concepts that Bryce had never even considered. He talked about desires and dreams and living in “right relationship” to others and to the earth.

His words were poetic, and Bryce found himself feeling peaceful and dreamy.

This hypnotic experience was suddenly shattered when Len Fernando asked if he could have a volunteer from the audience, and Topher, grabbing Bryce's elbow, shot his arm into the air. Len Fernando looked right at him.

"You," he said, pointing at Bryce.

Bryce was transfixed.

"Please stand up," Len Fernando directed.

"Yes sir," Bryce said, standing.

"When there is someone in our lives who elicits anger," Len Fernando explained, "we hope to avoid them, or even lash out at them, but we do not see them for who they truly are. A person that causes us pain or anger or any other negative emotion is a teacher. The more strongly we feel against them, the greater the lesson."

Bryce wondered where he fit into this scenario.

Len Fernando continued, "There is a great story from the eastern traditions about a monastery where one monk was hated by all the others. For years, they endured him, until one day he packed his belongings and left. When the leader of the monks was informed, he chased after the monk and urged him to return. Later, the other monks said to him, 'Why did you ask him to come back?' and the leader said, 'Because you will learn more from him than you ever could from me.'"

Bryce shifted his weight uncomfortably, hoping Len Fernando hadn't forgotten about him.

At that point, the shaman addressed him, saying, "Would you please say aloud the given name of someone towards whom you have recently felt great anger?"

All the men turned to look at him. Bryce's mind went blank, and then he remembered his heated exchange with Cricket.

"Cricket," he said. Immediately, there was a ripple of murmurs among the audience. Bryce wondered what he had done wrong. Technically, her given name was Kristen. Maybe he shouldn't have used the nickname.

It seemed like an eternity before Len Fernando said, "That is very auspicious. In traditional teachings, the cricket is a symbol of strong awareness and success. You could accept this symbol as an encouragement to learn from your interactions with this person, Cricket, who may awaken in you strong awareness and through whom you may achieve success. Do you feel you could try this?"

"Yes," said Bryce, almost to his own surprise.

"I see you have a question," Len Fernando said. He drew his mouth back into a sort of smile.

Bryce didn't know how he knew that, but he said, "You say that the fact that I feel anger towards her means there's a great lesson for me. I don't think I understand what the lesson is."

Len Fernando responded, "What form did your anger against her take?"

"I said a lot of angry things to her, because of insulting things she'd said to me," he explained.

Len Fernando said, "The Christian Bible makes reference to the tongue, and says that while it is such a small organ, it is almost beyond our power to tame it. Your anger at Cricket caused you to lose control over your own speech. That is a powerful lesson."

Bryce realized Len Fernando would love Tiffany.

After making a few more comments, Len Fernando indicated that Bryce could sit down again. Occasionally, men would glance over at him.

When the lecture was finished, the first thing Bryce did was ask Topher why the hell he had pushed his arm up.

"I figured you wanted to, but were too shy," Topher said. "I know *I* was at my first workshop. I wished someone had pushed my arm up, so that's why I did it to you. And that's pretty special that not only is Cricket your teacher, but the name has spiritual significance, too."

That reminded Bryce that he meant to bitch him out for giving Cricket his number, but something about the atmosphere of the place didn't lend itself to harsh criticism.

When the next session began, all the chairs had been cleared from the main hall and the men assembled. Don called everyone to attention. Harvey, one of the co-directors, spoke briefly about spirit animals and their place in native culture. He asked anyone who already knew their spirit animal to raise their hand.

Bryce was shocked to see about three-quarters of the attendees' hands in the air. Undoubtedly, these guys were not new to Native American spirituality, Bryce realized.

Harvey had all the people without spirit animals, like Bryce and Topher, line up against the wall. Meanwhile, Don and Little Bear formed the rest of the men into a circle. They took turns saying what their spirit animal was, and telling a little about how it affected their life.

After that, Little Bear brought out a drum and Len Fernando appeared. Harvey explained that Len Fernando was going to tell those without spirit animals which animal they were. After that, he would perform a ritual.

This time, they had all the men gather around the as-yet unaffiliated. Len Fernando stood in the midst of them while Little Bear began drumming. Len Fernando closed his eyes for a long time. Then he went to each man, paused a moment with his eyes closed, and told them their spirit animal.

When he got to Topher, he said "You are the rabbit, a harmless and spontaneous creature; you display both vulnerability and strength." Then he moved on to Bryce.

While standing before Bryce, it seemed he remained quiet longer than he had for the others.

Finally, he opened his eyes. Bryce thought Len Fernando had a surprised expression on his face.

"You are the owl," he said. This elicited some murmuring among the men. Nobody else had been an owl. He saw Don whisper something to Harvey.

"You see the hidden truth, for the owl sees what others miss," Len Fernando said. Then he surprised Bryce by whispering, "Come with me later."

Len Fernando finished telling the spirit animals of the rest of the men and then he went to stand by Little Bear, who continued drumming while he chanted a blessing over all the participants. The chant went on for several minutes. Len Fernando left. Then Don and Harvey sang some kind of song while Little Bear played on a different drum.

It was during this song that Bryce felt something tugging the back of his shirt. It was Len Fernando, who tipped his head towards a vacant room adjoining the main hall. They went in and Len Fernando shut the door.

"Why did you want to see me?" Bryce asked.

"Sometimes I am able to read people, and while I was sensing your spirit animal, I saw other things. Do you want to receive this information?" he asked.

Bryce felt like he was being asked if he wanted to accept a collect call.

He looked at Len Fernando for a moment before answering "Yes."

Len Fernando sat down in a chair and motioned for Bryce to do the same. Len Fernando closed his eyes and leaned forward as if he were praying.

"You have recently caused great harm; it was unintentional. Those whom you've hurt will forgive you," he said. Bryce figured that must mean Norm and Mattie. Suki had gone home from the hospital the next day. Bryce was glad to know the Fentons wouldn't hate him forever.

Len Fernando continued. "Your people are vanishing. They were once a great power, but now they grow fainter and fainter every day until they will be no more." Bryce knew that had to mean him and all other Old Money people.

"Now is the time for skillful action," Len Fernando said. "Now is the time to start running towards the future, to outrun your enemies, to get there before they do." Bryce didn't know what to make of that one.

Len Fernando sat back and said, "Is there anything you want to ask me?"

"How did you know I was an owl?" Bryce asked.

"Because I am an owl," Len Fernando said.

Len Fernando waited a moment and then he got up to leave.

"Do you have any advice for me?" Bryce asked.

"Drink lots of water," Len Fernando said. Then he left.

Back in the main hall, Bryce could smell garlic. Dinner was cooking. The song had just ended and the men were taking a break.

Bryce found Topher, who said that after the ceremony, it dawned on him that he had been at a Native American retreat months earlier and had already been told his spirit animal.

"What were you last time?" Bryce asked.

"I was a rabbit then, too," Topher answered.

Bryce was starving. He couldn't wait to see what the tribal cooks had prepared for their dinner. He wondered if it might be something with cranberries and pecans, and perhaps venison with rice and squash. The smell of garlic was growing more and more overpowering from the kitchen. He wasn't aware that Native Americans used garlic in their cooking, but then again, he didn't really know anything about tribal cuisine.

Finally, it was time for the buffet to begin. By the time Bryce got to the first station, he saw that the meal was composed of salad, garlic bread, and lasagna. Don was standing nearby.

"Don," Bryce said, calling him over, "This workshop has been really terrific, but I have to ask you something. With all the wonderful traditional foods your tribe must have, why are you serving lasagna?"

Don beamed. "Because everyone in the tribe loves pasta."

Bryce was amazed. The Dutch could've kept their beads. The whole of North America could've been theirs in exchange for a few trays of baked ziti.

After dinner, several men from Don's tribe showed up with drums and formed a large circle. Little Bear joined them. Everyone else gathered around. The men started drumming. Bryce had to admit, it produced a thunderous sound—the heartbeat of the earth, as Don explained.

Some of the men were moving their heads or tapping their feet. Topher started moving more and more as the drumming went on. By the time the drums stopped, he was completely rocking out.

"I told you that was going to be great; wasn't it?" Topher asked.

Before he could answer, Darryl and Aster appeared.

Aster said, "Can you feel the heart-energy in this room?" He was covered in perspiration. He had probably been dancing his ass off.

"Absolutely," said Topher.

"Well, we have a long way to go, so we should be getting on," Bryce said, hoping to extricate himself from their presence.

“I live in Westchester and Bryce lives in Connecticut on a big estate in the woods,” Topher said.

“Man, I love the woods,” Darryl said. “Being able to experience nature is the ultimate communion with Spirit.”

Topher had a sudden inspiration. “You should come to Bryce’s place sometime,” he said. “Maybe we can all get together again there.”

Aster said, “Bryce, that would be amazing. I cannot begin to describe what the woods do to me.”

Bryce had no intention of finding out.

“Topher,” Bryce said, handing him his car keys, “Why don’t you go warm up the car and I’ll give them my contact information.”

Topher took the keys and left.

Bryce gave his number to Darryl and Aster, making sure he had a temporary attack of dyslexia while he did so.

14

Susan called him on Sunday.

“What the hell did you do to the Fentons’ dog?” she asked.

She told Bryce that she and Patty had been brunching that morning with friends from Norfolk who’d heard it around town that Bryce had attempted to poison his neighbors’ dog.

“Everyone said it was no surprise since you’d already made it clear you were a dog-hater. The worst Grandfather ever did was to threaten to call the dog catcher on them. But you! Christ, what possessed you to kill her?” she asked.

“I didn’t try to kill her,” Bryce said. “It was all an accident. Everything will be fine.”

“You’ll be lucky if the Fentons don’t sue,” she countered.

Bryce explained the Fentons’ initial intrusion and his unsuccessful attempt to set boundaries, as well as the wood-splitting injury and finally, the inadvertent poisoning of Suki.

“Did you at least pay their vet bill?” Susan asked.

“It’s all taken care of,” Bryce assured her. “I even ordered some flowers and squeaky-toys and things to be sent around as a get-well gift for her.”

“No chocolates, I hope,” Susan said.

After he’d convinced her the Fentons weren’t going to descend upon him with a fleet of lawyers, he asked after the baby. Susan said she was doing very well, but that Patty was acting strangely.

“I think she’s the first adoptive mother who ever had post-partum depression,” she said. “Actually, I shouldn’t joke. It’s called post-adoptive depression. It’s a thing.”

"Is there anything I can do?" Bryce asked.

"I don't know. I've never seen her like this before. Maybe it'll all blow over," Susan said. She changed the subject. "What have you been up to this weekend?"

"I went to a Native American spiritual renewal workshop," Bryce said.

There was a pause. Bryce hoped Susan hadn't dropped the receiver.

"Bryce, tell me what's going on. First Father Jeff and now this?" Susan said.

"Okay," Bryce confessed. "Rosemary is very spiritual and she's currently mixed up with this priest who might be leaving the seminary for her, and I figured if I were more spiritually developed, she might be more attracted to me."

"Why can't you just buy her jewelry like everyone else?" Susan asked.

They talked about it a little longer and Bryce promised he wouldn't shave his head or take any religious vows without first consulting her.

"I don't know what you need all that nonsense for, anyway," Susan said. "Every time I hold my daughter, I know that there's a God."

There were also some very powerful attorneys involved, Bryce thought, but he didn't feel it would be the right time to point that out.

They said goodbye.

15

During the next week, Bryce thought about his experience at the workshop. Between that and his visit with Father Jeff, he was learning quite a bit about spirituality despite himself. He didn't feel particularly further along the road to enlightenment, but spiritual matters now held a certain philosophical appeal. He could see where a thinking man could feast on religious ideas alongside the saints. He began to vaguely classify himself as such a man.

On Wednesday morning, Tiffany called.

"Is Deek okay?" Bryce quickly asked.

"Deek's fine," she said. "Meet me for lunch."

Bryce was taken aback. Tiffany had never called him before. He ruled out any romantic interest immediately since she'd made it abundantly clear she thought he was a spoiled jerk. However, she'd developed a grudging tolerance for him as a second opinion, as it were, about rich-people matters. Whenever she distrusted or disagreed with something Deek or his family told her, she'd come to Bryce for verification, or to have him explain it in such a way that it might make more sense.

In answer to her question, Bryce said, "I will meet you if you ask me the right way."

There was a loud exhale of exasperation and then she said, “Will you please have lunch with me?”

“Yes,” Bryce responded. “I’d be delighted.”

“You can come here. I’m trying a new fancy chicken recipe from Deek’s mother. It uses those pity shells,” she said.

“*Patty* shells,” Bryce corrected.

“Whatever,” she snapped. “Are you coming or not?”

“No,” Bryce said, “But what I will do instead is take you out to lunch. Anywhere you’d like to go. My treat.”

“Anywhere?” she asked with incredulity.

Bryce’s mind reeled. Perhaps he’d opened the door to lunch at some hell-hole in the Bronx with Hamburger Helper on the menu, or worse, one of the trendy new places where everything was dripping with EVOO and served on a bed of quinoa. He braced for the worst.

“I want us to go to Lucky Duck,” she said haltingly. “But you gotta let me leave the tip.”

“Where is it?” Bryce asked.

“It’s not far from here. It’s Thai food,” she explained.

Bryce figured it sounded okay, so he said yes.

He picked her up at her apartment and they arrived at the restaurant soon thereafter.

“Hello, Tiffany!” the lady behind the front desk said when they walked in. She seemed ecstatic to see them. Bryce was surprised.

“Hey, Gamon,” Tiffany said.

“Today you bring a friend with you,” Gamon remarked.

“This is Bryce,” Tiffany said.

“Hello, Bryce!” Gamon said.

“How do you do?” Bryce said.

Gamon picked up two menus and led the way directly to a table in the back. The place was almost empty, which worried Bryce, but it was a nice little eatery.

“Your favorite table, Tiffany. Just for you. Enjoy your lunch!” Gamon exclaimed before going to the kitchen. Tiffany sat in the Gangster Seat, so named because it was the seat or seats in any restaurant in the back corners, where the diner sat with their back to the corner, presumably so they could see enemies approaching. Bryce wondered if she was being targeted by anyone, but figured she simply chose that seat from force of habit because of her previous life in rough neighborhoods.

As Tiffany removed her coat, she said to Bryce, “That’s Gamon. She’s the new owner. She bought this place from the owner of another Thai restaurant that had been here forever but was going out of business. It’s out of the way, so a lot of people don’t know about it, or they still think it’s the old place that wasn’t very good.” She continued, “Her name, Gamon, means ‘from the heart’ in Thai language. Isn’t that cool?”

“Interesting,” Bryce said. He was amazed that Tiffany had learned so much and ingratiated herself with the owner. He also knew that Deek didn’t care for Thai, so he suspected they’d never eaten here together.

Within seconds, a young woman appeared with two glasses of water and a plate heaping with hot crispy little spring rolls. She smiled at Tiffany and nodded her head.

Tiffany asked Bryce, “What do you want to drink?”

“I’d like some tea, please,” he said to the girl, who nodded again. Then the girl looked at Tiffany, who said, “The usual.”

Tiffany was crunching on a spring roll as Bryce looked over the menu. When the girl returned with Tiffany’s drink and Bryce’s tea, Tiffany told her “I’ll have the usual for lunch,” and said to Bryce, “Tell her what you want to eat.”

Bryce ordered a cup of Tom Yum soup and Basil Fried Rice with chicken.

When the girl was gone, Tiffany said, “That’s Kwang. She’s only been in America for a few months. Her English isn’t that great and she’s kind of shy, but she’s always nice to me.”

Tiffany took a sip of her drink. “You know what this is?” she asked.

Bryce knew, but he decided to let her educate him for a change.

“No, what is it?” he asked.

“It’s bubble tea,” she said. “It’s like a special kind of tea and they put these things in it,” she said, pointing to the bottom of her glass.

“Hmm,” Bryce said, pretending to study them, “I bet they’re made of tapioca.”

“No, they’re some kind of bubbles you can eat,” she said. Bryce had to bite his inner lip to keep from laughing.

Just then, Kwang returned with Bryce’s soup. She also brought a plate piled high with some kind of shrimp.

“Special just for you, Tiffany,” Kwang said, smiling, and then left.

“You wanna see something?” Tiffany asked, picking up her chopsticks and holding them properly.

Bryce feigned extreme admiration. "That's terrific," he said. "Wow, that's really something."

"Gamon taught me how to use them," Tiffany said with obvious pride. "Do you know how to use chopsticks?" she asked with what Bryce detected was a hint of superiority.

He would've liked to have told her that he'd been using them since the age of five, and that anyone who didn't know how to use them was a moron, but he realized that this moment was about making Tiffany feel good about her accomplishments in hopes she would be motivated to continue with her self-improvement.

"I do know how to use chopsticks but I'm not terribly good at it," he lied.

"The secret is that you have to keep practicing," she explained. "I probably spent an hour before I got good with it. There was food everywhere. Oh, and Gamon told me that you shouldn't ever use them like drumsticks to tap on your plate. That's really rude, so don't do that."

Bryce ate a spoonful of soup. He knew he'd choke on it, but it was better than laughing out loud. As he coughed into his napkin, Tiffany picked up a shrimp with her chopsticks and delicately ate it.

"I don't know what they put in these, but they're really good. I don't even order them, they just bring them to me. I told you they were nice," she said.

"So you come here on your own," he said to Tiffany. "Had you ever eaten Thai food before?"

"No," she said. "I didn't know what it was, but one day I was just passing and I decided to go in. Gamon told me about all the foods. She even showed me where Thailand is on a map. It's near China," she added for Bryce's benefit. He bit his lip again. He feared he wouldn't make it through lunch without maiming himself.

"Sometimes I just come here to have bubble tea because it's quiet and everyone is really nice," she said.

They talked about Tiffany's new apartment and how she was finding the area, and then Kwang appeared with two fragrant, steaming plates of food. Tiffany thanked her.

"You know what this is?" she asked Bryce, pointing at her lunch.

"No," he said, although he had a pretty good idea.

"It's called Pad Thai. It's this special kind of spaghetti with different vegetables and chicken, and you'll never guess what they put on top," she said.

"What?" Bryce asked, with mock suspense.

"*Peanuts*," she said. "Isn't that crazy? Putting peanuts on spaghetti? But it's so good. And look what else they put," she said, pointing to the side of her dish.

"Limes," he observed.

"It makes the spaghetti taste even better when you squish them all over everything," she said.

Bryce ate his lunch and wondered when she'd get around to whatever it was that had really prompted her to contact him. He decided to coax it along.

"So, how are things going with Deek's family?" he asked. He knew there had been some discussion about having certain of her visible tattoos removed. All things considered, Deek's mother had instituted what Bryce thought was a pretty lenient tattoo policy for her future daughter-in-law. Anything with skulls or thunderbolts had to go, but she could keep the flowers, hearts, and butterflies. Everyone in the upper crust was allowed to have some eccentricity, so that was going to be hers.

"They're making me get rid of my ink," she said, "And they're going to have some kind of teacher come to my apartment and work on how I talk and manners and stuff."

Tiffany looked glum. Bryce felt badly that she was having to undergo so much renovation, but surely, she must have realized when she became involved with Deek that she would have to make certain lifestyle changes.

"You know," Bryce began, "I'm sure we all seem very snobbish to you, and a lot of the things we do don't make sense, but believe me, you'll be better off in the end. More importantly, I think you'll begin to see that there are a lot of good reasons why we behave the way we do. Take speech, for example," he continued. "People are judged by the way they talk. Is that right? Is it fair? Probably not, but that's the reality. We can choose to speak incorrectly and have people disregard all the other good things about us as soon as they hear how we talk, or we can speak properly and get along with everyone."

"That's a bunch of sugar," she said.

"Really? I bet you'd do it too. Let's pretend you need to hire a maid. A woman shows up wearing flip-flops with a cigarette in her face, holding a can of beer. Another woman shows up neatly dressed with a list of glowing references, and ready to work. Which one are you going to hire?" he asked her.

"That's easy," Tiffany said, laughing. "I'm hiring the chick with the beer. We can drink and watch TV together."

Bryce realized he'd picked a bad example.

Suddenly, her mood became serious. "Bryce," she said, "I need to ask you if you think I can pull this off, because I don't know if I can." She looked up at him in dismay.

He'd never seen her so vulnerable before, but he realized she'd been hiding it better than anyone he ever knew. Other women cried when they were overwhelmed or afraid. Tiffany never shed a tear, and he suddenly made the sad deduction that people only cry when someone cares. Where Tiffany came from, being hurt didn't matter to anyone, so she didn't bother crying.

Bryce wasn't sure what to tell her. Her success depended entirely on her, so he felt he should make her aware of that.

"If you're asking me if it's possible for you to adjust to Deek's world, then I would say yes. It'll require you doing what Deek says and not being stubborn. It'll require you putting up with his mother and sisters and following their lead. You'll have to leave behind a lot of things you may have liked, but in exchange, you'll be living a life that most women would kill for. Are some people going to be unwilling to accept you? Yes, but don't take it personally. There are people who hate my sister and my friends and me. That's just the way it is. But if you take your self-improvement seriously and don't let anyone discourage you, I think you have what it takes."

"Really?" she asked.

"Look at this," he said, spreading his arms to indicate the dining room. "You've come to this place and learned about a new cuisine and made friends from a foreign country. You even learned to use chopsticks. That took a lot of courage. I think Deek would be very proud of you."

"Don't you tell Deek I come here," she said, practically jumping out of her seat. "This place is for me. I don't want him coming in here, telling me I'm not picking up my glass with the right hand or making fun of me because I never heard of some vegetable. When I'm here alone, I can be myself."

"That's just it," Bryce said. "You've done everything right because you've been kind and courteous and open-minded."

"I felt pretty bad after that gala," she said. "Stupid rich people. What a bunch of heavy furniture. They think they're all that and a bucket of ice cream. They can kiss my ass."

"What happened at that gala?" Bryce asked. "Did someone hurt you?"

Tiffany debated a minute before going on. "I was in the bathroom and some woman was talking about me and Deek. Mostly talking trash about me."

"Did you confront her?" he asked.

"No," she said.

"Tiffany, that's a huge step in the right direction. Do you know why? Because she made herself look like a fool speaking badly about you while you sailed through the evening without letting it get to you, and I guarantee you that Deek has tons more money than whoever she came with. She's probably so jealous she could spit," he said.

That explanation seemed to satisfy her. A little later she asked him why all the silver at Deek's parents' home had different initials on it.

"The forks have one letter, but the candle-holders have a different one, and I've seen all kinds of different initials on trays and other stuff. Is it because they can't afford to get their initials put on it?" she asked.

"I can see why you might think that, but you're dead wrong. The different initials are because the pieces have been inherited from various relatives. One of the easiest ways to tell new money is because all their silver has their own initials. They didn't have any rich relatives to inherit anything from."

"Oooooh," Tiffany said. "I think I'm starting to get this."

After lunch, Gamon brought them some sliced papaya sprinkled with shredded coconut and a plate of firm custard which had been cut into squares.

When Gamon presented Bryce with the bill, Tiffany snapped, "And remember, I'm paying the tip."

"I appreciate the gesture, but it's really unnecessary," he assured her.

"No, I insist, I'm leaving the tip," she said.

When they got outside after Gamon and Kwang had seen them off with many thanks and good wishes and entreaties to return very soon, Tiffany said to Bryce, "You know what I do with that money?"

Bryce was puzzled. "What money?" he asked.

"The thousand dollars Deek gave me to spend at the gala," she said.

Bryce vaguely remembered. "No, what do you do with it?" he asked.

"Every time I come here, I leave a fifty-dollar tip," she said.

Bryce smiled. "You have the makings of a philanthropist in you," Bryce said.

"Don't tell Deek," she said. "I don't want him knowing I'm nice."

"I think what you mean to say is that you don't want to show off your charity," Bryce said. "But if that's so, why did you tell me?"

"You don't count," Tiffany said.

16

Bryce was pretty sure it was Alistair Cooke who said that the clink of ice in glasses at sunset is the loveliest sound in the world.

It was Thanksgiving, and he was at Nathalie and Ben's, along with Susan and Patty and the baby. Nathalie's mother, Ingrid, had just returned from a Viking Cruise on the Rhine River, which she said was magnificent. She still hadn't decided where to live now that she'd given Nathalie and Ben the house, but there was time for that. Since being widowed by Minty's death, she was doing well. Bryce had invited Rosemary to join him, but she was having dinner in New York with relatives of her father who lived in Riverdale.

Polly had just served them a splendid holiday dinner which started off with her famous shrimp cocktail, a longtime favorite of Bryce's. Coffee and pie had been enjoyed half an hour ago. Now they were drinking cocktails and playing Charades. It was Susan's turn.

"Cat!" Nathalie correctly guessed. Susan touched her nose. It was part of a longer title of a book. Susan had tugged her ear before acting it out, so it was a word that sounded like "cat." The beginning of the title so far was "The Great."

"The Great Gatsby," Ingrid guessed. She was right. "Talk about *nouveau riche*!" Ingrid said. Everyone laughed.

Next, it was Bryce's turn. He liked Charades. He'd decided to act out "Merchant Ivory." He could pantomime an elephant for the second name, but the "Merchant" might be a little trickier.

He created an invisible counter in front of him and pretended to be handing things to customers.

"Ballet!" Nathalie called out.

"Robot," guessed Ben.

"You're a radical on a street-corner, passing out pamphlets," Susan said, provoking a few giggles.

"Assembly-line worker?" Ben suggested.

"No, he's a soup-kitchen worker. He's handing out bowls of soup," Patty said.

Bryce decided to skip "Merchant" for the time being and go on to the "Ivory" part. They guessed it in seconds. Then they went for the whole phrase.

"Scrimshaw ivory," Susan guessed.

"Merchant Ivory," Ben announced. Bryce touched his nose.

They all decided to take a break. The baby was getting fussy and Patty was going to bring her home to Margaret. Susan told her she should've been in bed hours ago, but Patty said she just wanted to make the most of her first Thanksgiving.

"Alexandra won't remember any of it, but years from now, we'll all remember how cranky she was," Susan said. Patty frowned at her and left. It was becoming obvious that their different approaches to parenting had created an ever-growing rift between them.

"You'll figure out a way to compromise," Ingrid said quietly to Susan, as she came and sat beside her. "Minty and I fought because he didn't want to send Nathalie away to boarding school. He got his way about that, but I got to pick her college. It's a constant battle, though."

"Bryce," said Ben, walking over to him, "Can I get you another drink?"

"No thanks, I'm fine," Bryce answered.

"Did you watch 'Friendly Persuasion' this morning?" Ben asked. It was invariably broadcast every Thanksgiving Day on some channel. Ben was a film buff.

“Not this year, but pretty much every other year. When we were children, they always put it on to keep us occupied when we had big family gatherings. It kept us from pestering the adults while they were talking,” Bryce explained.

“The first time I ever saw it was last year,” Ben said. “I don’t know how appropriate it is for children, though. That film’s pretty suggestive.”

“Suggestive? How?” Bryce asked.

“Gary Cooper is always giving his wife smoldering glances, and then there’s that scene where he and his wife have a roll in the hay—you know, the barn scene?” Ben said.

Bryce thought about it. “You’re right,” he said. “Come to think of it, it probably wasn’t the most wholesome choice for children, but I guess we didn’t know what to make of it. I just remember the goose.” Ben laughed.

The topic of holiday television broadcasts made Bryce think of something Ben might find interesting.

“Have you seen the Yule Log yet?” Bryce asked.

“Is it something you bought for Christmas?” Ben asked, taking a sip of his scotch.

“No,” he explained, “I don’t mean it like a decoration or a cake—I’m talking about the one on TV.”

“No, I don’t,” Ben said, becoming visibly interested.

“Well, years ago, I think it was in the seventies,” Bryce began, “this TV station here in New York started broadcasting what they called the Yule Log, on Christmas Day. Since so many people in the city live in apartments and don’t have a fireplace, and maybe they were having family or friends over for Christmas dinner, what they would do—and this is back in the days when they had the big TVs that were a piece of furniture, with the feet—they’d leave that on all day. The broadcast started on Christmas morning and all it showed was a log in a fireplace.”

“Just a log?” Ben asked.

“Yes, a log that was burning,” Bryce told him. “And meanwhile, in the background, there were Christmas carols and other festive holiday music playing. This way, the poor could have a fireplace and musical entertainment in their tiny apartments to make Christmas nice for their guests. It was probably intended for them, but of course, everyone watched the Yule Log. We always had it on, too.”

“I’ll definitely check it out this year. That sounds really cool,” Ben said.

“It is,” Bryce assured him.

Ah, the Yule Log, thought Bryce. Soon it would be Christmas.

The rest of the evening passed peacefully enough, until finally he returned to Susan's house, where he would be spending the night. Margaret's son John was over, helping her get the Christmas decorations out of storage, as they would have to go up on Sunday, in time for the first day of Advent. John was also charged with taking delivery of the tree and greenery on Saturday. It was lucky for them that he was a strapping young man.

Bryce popped into the kitchen to wish them goodnight and say that he hoped they'd had a happy Thanksgiving. John was sitting at the kitchen table doing some kind of homework, and Margaret was setting up a breakfast casserole for the morning. They wished him a good night, also.

After he'd settled in bed, Bryce could hear Susan and Patty arguing. Patty was becoming loud. Usually, Susan was the louder of the two, but Bryce reflected on how Susan had said Patty was suffering from post-adoptive depression. Bryce had noticed she was definitely becoming irritable, and she was growing thin. She'd never been a big eater, but she was starting to look tired and sickly. Susan had suggested that the two of them take a trip to Saratoga for the baths and spa. Susan swore by the water from the natural springs, but Patty wouldn't touch the sulfur-rich water, which she said smelled objectionable.

In the morning, Patty didn't come down for breakfast. Susan excused her absence, saying she wasn't feeling well, but Bryce guessed it had to do with the previous evening's fight.

As he and Susan enjoyed Margaret's casserole, Susan told him that she was looking forward to getting a lot of miscellaneous tasks done next week. Patty would be going to visit her parents for a couple of weeks and she was taking Alexandra with her. Patty's family would have plenty of time with the baby, and it would give Patty a chance to recharge and hopefully, to return in a better mood. Bryce agreed it sounded like a good plan.

As he drove back to Connecticut, Bryce was somewhat dysphoric. He didn't know why, but something seemed amiss.

Thinking back to the workshop, he remembered what Len Fernando had said privately to him about his people vanishing. How could that be? So much had gone into creating his family and the families of those around him. They had been raised from the seeds of their forefathers' ambition, fortified with the best sustenance in secure surroundings, cultivated with care, and sheltered from the harsh wind.

Bryce knew, however, that change was affecting families like his. Already in Europe, as his friend Cristina frequently explained, the rich were no match for the super-rich.

Bryce remembered something else Len Fernando had said, and resolved that somehow, he would have to outrun his enemies. The future depended upon it.

PART TWO

17

Rohan's laugh was a sound that always cheered Bryce. It had been quite some time since he'd seen him. They were lunching at an Indian restaurant in the Upper East Side, where Rohan lived.

The son of a wealthy Brahmin cashew farmer, Rohan had just returned from India, where he had narrowly escaped marrying a horrible woman, the details of which he recounted to Bryce. Soon afterwards, their lunch was served.

"So how are things down on the farm?" Bryce asked.

"My family is trying again to find me a wife," he reported.

"I'm sure they'll be a little more circumspect this time," Bryce said. Rohan's ex-fiancée was a cruel and stupid young woman who, fortunately, became impregnated by someone else during their engagement, so his family was able to break the agreement.

"Definitely," Rohan assured him. "No more girls from new-money families. My parents learned their lesson. They only agreed to that match because her parents were so eager to gain respectability. Afterwards, they regretted it. Her father—all he did was brag about all his money and status. My family couldn't stand him. This time they are trying for a match with a girl from a family like ours. Maybe not super-rich, but at least she will have some class. How about you? You said you are seeing this woman named Rosemary?"

"It's not going that well. She's possibly still in love with a man who's studying to be a priest," Bryce said.

"Man, what is it with you and these crazy girls?" Rohan asked, his quirky laugh beginning to ascend.

"She's not crazy," Bryce said. "She's just confused. She needs time."

"She needs her head examined," Rohan said, taking a bite of Tandoori Chicken. "Then again, so do you, running around poisoning dogs. You're mad, do you know that?"

Bryce waited until Rohan's giggles subsided.

"I did not poison her," Bryce said flatly. "It was an accident."

"A whole bloody chocolate bar?" Rohan said, his laughter rising in crescendo.

"How was I to know?" Bryce said.

"Hey, Bryce, my friend, let me ask you this: do you know where the town well is?" Rohan asked.

Bryce frowned. "I'm not sure. Why?"

"Try not to go throwing any rat poison down there. It will make everyone die." Rohan was hunched forward over his plate, convulsing with snickers.

"I'll try to remember," Bryce said.

"No, seriously, because if you get yourself in trouble, I'm not coming to help you. You think I'm going to get my face on the news? No way!" Rohan was positively consumed with glee.

Just then, Bryce saw a blonde woman several tables away turn to look because Rohan was creating a bit of a stir with his laughter. When he recognized her, he felt his stomach tense up immediately. It was Cricket.

She was far enough away that he could pretend he hadn't seen her. He wondered if she'd recognized him. He put his face down and concentrated on moving his fork around vigorously in his Aloo Gobi. He watched carefully out of the corner of his eye as she turned back to face the woman with whom she was dining.

"Rohan," he whispered, "I've just been spotted. We need to get out of here."

"What?" Rohan asked mirthfully, "The authorities have finally tracked down Bryce Parnell, the homicidal poisoner?"

"No, no," Bryce hissed pleadingly. "It's that woman—over there—the blonde."

"Ah! Another one of your crazy women!" Rohan said, obviously delighted by the prospect of a fresh source of amusement.

"She's crazy, all right," Bryce said. "She's been after me for ages."

"Does she want to jump your bones?" Rohan guffawed.

"No, she's on some committee—" Bryce began explaining.

"Look out, here she comes!" Rohan said.

Bryce prayed that Rohan was only kidding him, but sure enough, a second later, there stood Cricket.

"Well, well, Bryce. Fancy meeting you here," she said. Her straight hair was cut in a blunt bob and she had more freckles than any adult he'd ever met.

"The food is simply magnificent, don't you think?" he asked her.

"I wish I could say the same for the clientele," she quipped, staring him down. "I bet they only let you in because of your friend here." She nodded in Rohan's direction.

"Me?" Rohan asked, placing his hand on his chest and feigning shock. "I'm an Aussie. I come from the land down under."

"So," she said smugly, "What have you been up to lately that's so much more important than your responsibilities?"

Before Bryce could answer, Rohan intervened.

"You didn't hear?" he asked her.

"Hear what?" Cricket asked.

"About the tumor," Rohan said.

"Tumor?" she asked.

"That's our Bryce," Rohan said, reaching across the table to grab one of his hands. "A true gentleman. He suffers in silence."

"What are you talking about?" Cricket asked.

Bryce realized he was at a crossroads. He wondered how she had the gall to confront him in a restaurant. She seemed very sure of herself, but then again, she always did. He could go with Rohan's desperate bid for sympathy and they could have a good laugh about it afterwards, but he knew that wouldn't really solve his problem, grateful thought he was to Rohan for making the attempt. On the other hand, he could sort it out once and for all. He remembered what Len Fernando had said about her being a teacher. He was ready to learn the ways of success.

"Cricket," he said, "My friend is pulling your leg. I'm fine. I simply have no interest in dealing with you ever again."

Cricket shook her head. "You really think you can get away with this?"

"I'm not trying to 'get away with' anything. You and the organization you represent are outdated, snobbish, pathetic, and irrelevant. I've tried to make that clear in the past, but you didn't seem to get the message, so I apologize for being so direct."

To Bryce's astonishment, Cricket was unfazed. She really thought she and her way of life was invincible.

"Someone certainly seems to think they're important," she laughed. "It's you who's going to be irrelevant after I get through telling—"

Bryce cut her off. "You're free to tell anyone anything you wish. Anyone who knows you will realize that whatever you're saying is nothing more than a shameless, futile attempt to exert the level of control that you wish you actually had."

"I take exception to that characterization," Cricket shot back. "My family owns—"

Bryce interrupted her again. "I didn't come here to listen to you talk about your department stores. They're of no interest to me. I also didn't come here to be accosted by someone who aspires to be on my level. I'll save you a lot of time by giving you some valuable advice: don't bother; you're not even close. Please go back to your small-minded friend and enjoy your mulligatawny soup before it gets cold."

"And please, if you're ever in Sydney, look me up," Rohan added.

As Cricket turned her back to them and strode to her table, Bryce felt a sense of relief. He'd told her what he thought. He'd been honest and straightforward for a change. He was upset to think of how frank he'd been, but he also acknowledged that with someone as rude as Cricket, he needed to make a definitive statement. He probably could've refrained from being unkind; in retrospect, that was wrong, but overall, the encounter was positive and freeing.

"I hate to say this," Rohan said, looking after her, "But she's very attractive, that crazy woman."

"She's married," Bryce informed him. "Besides, she lives in a world the size of a matchbox. She's from one of those self-important old families. You know, the kind that discriminates against other old families they think are less important."

"You mean her people had better seats on the Mayflower than yours?" Rohan asked.

"Something like that," Bryce said. "They're just a bunch of moldy old skinflints with a pedigree. Their heads are pretty far up their own backsides."

Cricket and her lunch date left. They both scowled in Bryce's direction. In an act of spontaneous humor, he made an ugly face and stuck his tongue out at them.

Rohan erupted into such a thunderous spasm of laughter that everyone in the restaurant turned to look.

18

Two days later, Bryce received a call from Aunt Bitsy. He imagined she wanted him to get tickets for them to see a pre-holiday showing of *The Fantasticks*, as they did every December. It marked the low point in his cultural year as he couldn't stand the musical, but he endured it willingly for Aunt Bitsy's sake since she had been such a dear friend of his late mother and had become a stand-in mother to him and Susan.

"Have you spoken to your sister?" she asked with a tone of concern in her voice.

"I was there last week for Thanksgiving," he replied.

"Bryce, Patty's taken the baby and gone to King of Prussia," she reported.

"Oh that," Bryce said. "Susan told me about that. She's visiting her family for a few weeks."

"No," Aunt Bitsy said. "She's absconded with the child."

Bryce couldn't remember the last time he'd heard anyone use the word "absconded."

Bryce laughed.

"She's just gone for an extended visit, Aunt Bitsy," he reassured her. "Susan was fine with it."

"Susan called me last night. She'd received a call from Patty saying she was never coming back," Aunt Bitsy said. "You must go to Susan immediately. She's at her wit's end."

“They’ve been fighting a lot lately,” Bryce said. “It’s probably just a tiff brought on by the stress of new parenthood. I’m sure they’ll work things out like they always do.”

“Patty has filed for divorce,” Aunt Bitsy said gravely.

Bryce was taken aback. He knew his sister-in-law often felt cowed by Susan’s domineering manner, but she knew Susan loved her, and despite their disagreements, Patty was extremely devoted to her. Running away with the baby seemed like a desperate act, and Bryce could hardly fathom Patty doing such a thing.

“I know Patty’s been going through a rough time; emotional stuff about being a new mother. Susan told me,” Bryce said. “She’ll probably call the whole thing off as soon as she calms down. Her family will help her see reason.”

“Her family has sent a barrage of lawyers down Susan’s throat,” she said bitterly. “Patty is demanding full custody and hoping to dismantle their prenuptial agreement.”

Upon hearing that, Bryce realized that Patty was spinning out of control. Whatever anger and pain she was feeling had driven her straight over the rails of common sense.

“Maybe Susan and I could go down there and try to talk with her,” Bryce said.

“You can’t,” Aunt Bitsy informed him. “She’s taken out a restraining order on Susan.”

“What?” Bryce exclaimed. “How can that even be? There’s no legal basis.”

“Bryce, her family is one of the oldest and most powerful families in Pennsylvania. They can do anything they want. That’s why this is so devastating. Susan knows what she’s up against,” Aunt Bitsy said.

Bryce was reeling. He’d never before had the need to judge between the relative power of his family and Patty’s, but he was trying to get a handle on the situation.

“But surely, if Patty’s serious, we’ve got the resources to fight this,” Bryce said.

Aunt Bitsy hesitated a moment before answering. “I hate to have to speak this way about your father, but as your mother told me many times, he never achieved the success of which he was so capable, especially with your grandfather Parnell’s help. Your grandfather had been very successful, as was his father before him, but your mother confided in me that your father didn’t pull his weight in the family, so to speak. A lot of important connections were missed and a lot of opportunities to advance the family financially were neglected,” she explained. “Susan has taken up the torch and done a marvelous job, but there was quite a bit of shortfall to make up for. She simply couldn’t do it all, especially when it would’ve been her place—and yours—to build your own layer upon your father’s legacy.”

“So what you’re saying is that we’re basically still catching up to get to where father should have been?” Bryce asked.

“Exactly,” Aunt Bitsy said.

"But Susan has money—I have money. We've got good lawyers. We can manage," he said.

"Not against a family like Patty's. They're formidable people, Bryce. I'm telling you," she said.

Bryce thought about Patty's parents, who were so nondescript as to be practically invisible, and her three brothers, who looked like something right out of a copy of *Boy's Life*. They were so unpretentious they actually wore Dockers. They seemed like reasonable people.

"Weren't her family Quakers a million years ago?" Bryce asked. He knew Quakers could be counted upon to behave sensibly.

"Her family made a fortune in plate glass," Aunt Bitsy said. "Patty is a sixth-generation trust recipient. Don't confuse religion and money. I always had a feeling that she wasn't a good match for Susan, and now she's in a position to financially cripple her and take the baby."

Bryce promised Aunt Bitsy he would go to Susan's at once.

When he arrived, Margaret let him in with her usual professionalism but he could tell she was troubled.

Before he could ask her how Susan was, he heard Susan in the study, raising her voice on the phone.

"Her lawyer," Margaret simply said, returning to the kitchen. Bryce remained standing in the front hall.

When Susan emerged, she was practically glowing with rage. Bryce knew better than to attempt physical contact when she was like this. She was in battle-mode.

"What's this all about?" he said, following her to the sitting room.

"She blindsided me, that's what she did," Susan said angrily. "The minute she arrived at King of Prussia, she called and told me she was staying. Running back home to mother because she didn't get her way. I saw no reason to give in on the nanny issue, so I told her to stop being foolish. Two days later, her legal team is all over me. I just got off the phone with Seth. He said she could actually make good on her threats."

"Have you tried talking to her?" Bryce asked.

"That's just it," Susan said, starting to look bewildered. "I called her last night and said I was sorry. I told her we could have three nannies if she wants. I was willing to negotiate with her, but she was so angry—I couldn't believe it."

Bryce sighed. He was truly sad to hear what had happened. He didn't know what to say.

"Susan," he said, "You know I love you, but you can be very rough on the people around you. I don't think you realized how much you were hurting Patty."

"Hurting? All I've ever done is try to make her happy," she exclaimed, indicating the walls. "Her goofy artistic photographs are all over the house. I almost sacrificed my relationship with Grandfather for her. We adopted Alexandra. She's ungrateful, that's what she is," she concluded.

Bryce knew Susan wouldn't value his opinion, but for what it was worth, he decided to share it anyway.

"You know what I think?" he said. "I think Patty puts up with a lot of things because she loves you, but maybe now that her emotions are on edge since the baby came, she's lashing out instead of holding it in. Just sit tight for a while and it'll all blow over."

Susan exploded on him.

"Blow over? What are you talking about? I'm facing an impossible legal situation and I'm going to lose Patty and the baby."

Bryce realized the depth of her despair because she did something he'd only seen her do twice before in her life: she broke down crying. It would be short-lived, he knew, but it was excruciating for him to watch. He handed her his handkerchief. A moment later, she had composed herself. She took a deep breath.

"You've still got me," Bryce said.

"Oh, *thanks*," she said sarcastically, but he knew she was comforted.

"It goes without saying that you can have everything I've got," he told her.

She considered him for a moment before responding.

"You're so dumb," she said. "Never give your money to someone in trouble."

"You'd do the same for me," he said.

"I'm not so sure about that," she said, but he knew she was kidding. At least he hoped she was. With Susan, you could never be entirely sure.

19

After he returned home, Bryce called Patty. They'd always been close and he felt sure he could help her reconcile with Susan, or at least get the process started.

He was terribly unprepared for the woman he reached on the other end of the line.

Patty was hysterical. She couldn't stop criticizing Susan. She alternated between self-pity for what she'd endured, and indignation, as she vowed she would never let Susan near her or the baby again.

Bryce remained calm and let her talk, but her irrationality unnerved him. This was going to be much worse than he thought. Maybe Susan was right.

He tried telling her that Susan was sincerely sorry and that she loved her and missed the baby.

"Patty, you know I wouldn't lie to you. This has nothing to do with the legal stuff. Susan's brokenhearted," he said.

"Bryce, I'm sorry, but you're just as oblivious as she is sometimes," she shot back. "I'm not going to raise my daughter in that claustrophobic snob-stronghold that you all love so much. I want her to live a full life without worrying what people say. She needs to feel supported, and that'll never happen as long as Susan's in the picture."

Bryce didn't understand a thing she said.

"But you're the one who wanted her to have a French nanny; you've taken her there to raise her at your parents' home. I don't mean to be unkind, but it's not like you're taking her to a commune. What's so different between there and here?"

"My family *accepts*, okay? They don't make demands," she said.

Bryce was starting to get the picture. Aunt Bitsy had always said that Patty was apt to be a spendthrift, and that she was more than a bit spoiled around the edges. She wanted Sandy to have the best of everything and Susan had obviously reigned her in. Also, the Robinsons were more flexible than the Parnells when it came to things like Patty choosing to be an artist and coming out as a lesbian. The Parnells eventually accepted things like that, but they weren't particularly receptive at first.

Bryce also recalled a conversation he'd had with Patty at Sandy's christening party where she said she wanted Sandy to meet all kinds of people.

"So this is about Sandy being able to live a broader life than what you and Susan currently have?" Bryce said.

"Finally, you're starting to get it," she said in a tone of exasperation he'd never heard her take with him before.

"Patty, I apologize if I've ever said or done anything to upset you. You know I love you like a sister. I'm sorry I didn't understand about why you left, but I do now. I can talk to Susan. I know if I explain—"

Patty cut him off. "Susan is incapable of understanding. She lives in denial of the feelings of others and even if she could understand, she wouldn't care. She'd want her way because that's the way it always is. Bryce, your sister is a terrible, terrible person. You need to know that."

Patty was incensed. Rather than calming down, she seemed to become more angry the longer they talked. Bryce decided it would be smart to end the conversation before things got any more heated. He tried to be upbeat.

"Patty, we all love you very much and I'm sure something can be worked out. In the meantime, you can always talk to me. I'm here for you," he said.

"Then you can tell Susan in no uncertain terms that it's over and that she is never going to see Sandy again. I'm not letting her ruin her life like she ruined mine," Patty said emphatically, and hung up.

Bryce stared at the receiver. Patty was insane. The connection they'd always shared had somehow vanished. She spoke to him like an enemy. He was wounded by her fury and shocked at her vindictiveness. Where was the warm bohemian sister-in-law he'd always known and loved?

He knew that whatever happened, Susan would survive. She was just that kind of person, like Grandfather. They were unstoppable. But he hated to think of her being hurt. As for Patty, whatever impression he'd had of her, it was clear she was someone else entirely, someone whose emotions were running amok and dictating her behavior. Bryce had always been taught that was a dangerous way to operate, and now he understood why.

He knew that no matter what, Sandy would be well cared for. However, he wondered if he would still be her godfather if Patty and Susan divorced.

Is there such a thing as an ex-godfather? he wondered. So few people in his circle were divorced that it carried with it a lot of unfamiliar implications. Divorce was messy, embarrassing, and expensive. People avoided it at all costs.

Suddenly, Bryce was starving. He decided to call for Chinese take-out. After he'd placed his order, he opened the front door to leave and found Suki on his doorstep.

"Hi, Suki," he said. She wagged her tail and bumped her nose into his leg.

He knew dogs were a lot smarter than they looked, so he said, "About the thing with the candy—I didn't know. Really. I'm sorry I made you sick." He leaned down and patted her under the chin. She licked his hand.

He went back into the house and called the Fentons. Bryce explained that he had to leave to pick something up, but that Suki would probably stick around. Maddie said not to worry, as she'd be over in a moment to get him. Bryce understood now that Suki's escapes were a ritual, not a catastrophe.

"See you next time," he said to Suki before he got in his car and drove off.

20

"Bryce, great to hear from you," Gabe said heartily.

Later that day, Bryce had decided to call since he knew how close Gabe was to Patty. Maybe he could offer some insight into her state of mind.

"Hi Gabe, I hope this won't be an awkward call. I was hoping to find out if you'd talked to Patty recently," he explained.

"Patty?" Gabe said. "Yes, as a matter of fact I have, but there's nothing awkward about it. She's left your sister."

"What I mean is, do you get the feeling she's serious?" Bryce asked.

"What do you think?" Gabe asked.

"I don't know," Bryce said. "I think there's a chance she might change her mind once she calms down."

"Well, I'm not a gambler," Gabe said, "But I wouldn't put money on it."

"You think she's really going to go through with all of this?" Bryce asked.

"Yes, definitely," Gabe said. "She's had it. She's through. And most important of all, this is about her child's future."

"I have to be honest," Bryce said, "I'm failing to see what she considers so terrible about our family when hers is basically the same."

"I'd have to agree with you there," Gabe said.

"Then you don't understand what this is all about either?" Bryce said, feeling somewhat comforted to hear it.

"Frankly, I haven't really thought much about it," he said. "All I know is that Patty's made up her mind, and when she does that, there's no chance she'll change it."

At least he's straightforward, Bryce thought.

"Listen," Gabe said, "Let's have lunch. We can talk about your nonprofit."

Bryce had been so focused on the situation with Patty that he completely forgot that Gabe had been touted as someone who could help him with his work.

"I'm free tomorrow," Bryce offered. "Where are you?"

"I'm here, I'm there, I'm everywhere," Gabe said, laughing. Bryce thought he could hear a woman giggling in the background.

Bryce suggested an Italian place in Ardsley. He hadn't been there in ages. They agreed to meet at noon.

The next day, Bryce entered the restaurant to find Gabe seated in one of the back corners.

He sits in the Gangster Seat, just like Tiffany, he thought. Then he remembered Susan telling him something about his having grown up in rough conditions. It was probably a holdover. At least he was wearing his sunglasses on top of his head this time. The restaurant had somewhat dim lighting.

When they shook hands, Bryce noticed Gabe's extravagant cologne again. He'd have to ask him what it was, but he felt sure it would be so outrageously expensive that he'd never buy it.

Just then, the waitress came over with a glass of wine for Gabe and asked Bryce what he would like.

"Pepsi, please," Bryce told her.

"Thanks so much, Totti," Gabe said. Clearly, he had wasted no time in getting to know the waitstaff.

"So tell me, Bryce," Gabe asked, "What is your goal for this nonprofit of yours?"

"At the moment, the challenge is finding donors. I'd like it to be a multifaceted charity that funds a variety of causes," Bryce said. "Overall, it's about fighting injustice."

Gabe nodded. "You know you're going to have to come up with an angle to get people on board, right?"

Bryce was puzzled. "What do you mean?" he asked.

"People who have money don't concern themselves with those problems—justice, ethics, starving kittens. Ignoring that stuff leaves them more bandwidth to process their own ambitions," Gabe said. "In order to get them to open their wallets, you have to give them something, because they don't believe in giving something for nothing."

Bryce remembered that all the congregants who gave large sums towards the repair of the church roof had their names announced in church by Father Jeff, and a couple had their surnames inscribed on a tablet on one of the sanctuary walls. It occurred to Bryce that Gabe was probably right.

"You know one of the best fundraising tactics ever? It's those setups where a portion of the proceeds of a sale for some high-end merchandise goes to the charity," Gabe said. "Rich women love that stuff. It gives them an excuse to overspend. If you can find a way to legitimize—or even better—reward their greed, you've got it made."

Bryce was finding himself put off by Gabe's coarse way of speaking. There was something unbecoming about it, even if it had a ring of truth.

Gabe must've intuited Bryce's thoughts, because suddenly, he laughed. "I didn't mean to shock you," he said. "You're probably not used to this kind of talk. It comes from growing up in Southie."

"Yes, my sister told me something about your family having fallen upon hard times," Bryce said.

"'Fallen upon hard times'?" Gabe repeated sarcastically, "Hard times fell on us. They fell damn hard."

At that moment, Totti appeared with Bryce's drink and took their order. Bryce was grateful for the interruption because he feared Gabe was antagonized by the topic of his upbringing, but as soon as they were done ordering, he continued his story.

"I grew up in a very privileged environment," Gabe said. "My siblings and I went to private school. We had a small yacht. We used to go sailing. We spent the summers in New Hampshire, and in the wintertime, we had a great big Christmas tree in the front room, all lit up, with lots of presents for everyone underneath it. And then one day, my father walked out on us, but believe it or not, that wasn't the worst thing. The worst thing was finding out that we'd lost everything. We couldn't even cover all of his gambling debts."

"Did you ever find him?" Bryce asked.

"Who cares?" Gabe said dismissively, and went on. "We learned pretty quickly that nobody was going to help us except for my grandmother's sister's family, so we moved to South Boston, where they were. My mother took a job as a cleaning woman because that was all she could get, but mostly we were on welfare once her health started fading. All of us kids went to public school and I got beat up more times than I can count. Back in Duxbury, my sister took violin lessons and my younger brother was on the chess team; I had been at the top of my class in Latin, and suddenly here I was, playing basketball after school with guys who put their guns on the benches on the sidelines while we played."

"They had guns?" Bryce asked incredulously. Gabe laughed.

"Yes, they had guns," he said. "And pretty soon I learned how to get along in that environment. I found work whenever I could to bring some money home, but I was lucky. I adapted. My mother just gave up. She died of cancer when I was in high school. And while I was putting myself through college, my older brother died of a drug overdose."

"I'm so sorry," Bryce said.

"Not as sorry as I am," Gabe said. "But once I'd graduated and started my career, I was careful enough with my money that I was able to make a lot of successful investments that allowed me to return to my old life. Amazingly, nothing had changed. The charity ball season still ran from September to May, and the maid's day off was still Thursday. What a nice, safe, structured little life it is."

Listening to him speak, Bryce realized he was looking at a man who was a modern-day Dickens. Just like the great writer who'd gone from a genteel existence to living with his family in debtor's prison and working ten hours a day in some kind of factory, Gabe had fallen from the pinnacle of society to the slums. Bryce knew that kind of experience did horrible things to a person. Dickens' novels were filled with bitterness towards the cruel treatment of the poor and the desperate unfairness of life. Somehow, Gabe, like Dickens, had returned from the abyss, but he was a freakish social oddity; a hybrid of very rich and very poor. There was something frightening about him which Bryce could not quite describe.

Gabe's mood mellowed when their lunch was served and he told an amusing story about the painter he'd recently hired to do a portrait of him.

"He was a poor kid from Buffalo who came to New York City to get into the art scene. The only work he could find at the time was doing sketches of people on the streets, you know, tourists mostly. He did that for years and obviously, the more he did, the more he got paid, so he learned to work very quickly and he really developed a talent for capturing people's personality, which is why he became such a great portraitist," Gabe said. "So one time when he and his wife were in Chicago, they were on their way back to their hotel after dinner one night when they got mugged. They went to the police station and the cop on duty tells him they'll get a police sketch artist to take the description of the mugger, but the painter whips out a pastel portrait he did of the guy. Can you believe it? It was so accurate, the cop instantly recognized the guy and they hauled him in. Isn't that a riot?" Gabe said.

"That mugger certainly picked the wrong person," Bryce said.

"From then on, he only mugged the blind," Gabe said.

"I've heard you travel quite a bit," Bryce said.

"I do business in different parts of the world, mostly China and Sweden," Gabe said. "I especially like Sweden. They have a very healthy society."

"They're socialists, aren't they?" Bryce said.

"They have a constitutional monarchy and they're a mixed economy, heavy on the exports. They practice mostly free market economics and have higher taxes than here, but very generous government entitlement programs that greatly enhance the quality of life for their citizens. They don't have minimum wage laws, but they don't need them because employers treat their workers fairly. In other words," Gabe said, taking a sip of his wine, "they're civilized."

"I'd always heard good things about Sweden," Bryce said.

"As a society, they believe very strongly in equality and individualism," Gabe said.

"I couldn't agree more," Bryce said.

Gabe smiled broadly. "Your belief in egalitarianism ends where the first-class ticket-holder line begins," he said. Before Bryce could say anything, he added "but that's to be expected because you're a product of your environment."

Bryce thought a moment before responding, "I can't claim to have had the same experiences you did, but I did walk away from my family for a time, and I know what it's like not to have money and to find yourself in trouble and there's nothing you can do."

"I realize that. Patty told me you were one of the good ones," Gabe said. "That's why you're trying to start this charity. Your heart's in the right place."

"Very much so," Bryce agreed enthusiastically. "And I'm learning all the time about different people and the issues that affect them. As it so happens, one of my friends is engaged to a woman from Co-op City, and she's opened my eyes to quite a number of things. For example, she told me about a cousin of hers who just purchased a house and has a 30-year-mortgage. Can you believe that? I didn't even know they existed."

Bryce took a bite of his Veal Scallopini. Gabe didn't say anything, but Bryce thought he saw a look of disgust in his eyes. Bryce reasoned that as an economist, the thought of anyone being stupid enough to have a 30-year-mortgage probably shocked him.

Bryce continued. "A lot of the problems of the poor are simply of their own making, but they do unquestionably face legitimate hardships. If I can help out where it counts, and especially, educate them about how to do better, I think they can succeed. It's all about getting them to see the big picture."

Gabe's interest appeared to have been piqued.

"And how do you define the big picture?" he asked.

Bryce said, "Society needs everyone to play their role in order for things to work, and if we all do the best we can and eliminate as many hinderances as possible, people will thrive. Society will thrive."

"What's your role in society?" Gabe asked. "Are you there to help eliminate those hinderances?"

"Yes—exactly," Bryce said. "I used to believe that if people were cold and hungry, you gave them blankets and soup. But Tiffany—this girl I was telling you about—said that if you do that, you'll just have to keep doing that. I even suggested projects like exposing the poor to the arts, in order to inspire them, but she told me that wouldn't address the issue either."

"What if I told you that Tiffany was right?" Gabe said. "And what if I told you that you're the one who hasn't seen the big picture?"

Bryce was slightly miffed by his remark. Gabe seemed to be implying that he knew all about how to cure society's ills.

"But I have," Bryce said. "Everyone says the rich are so advantaged, and our privilege is what gets us ahead. Fine. Then let me share my privilege with others. Let me give them a hand as they climb the ladder."

"Bryce, as I said before, your heart's in the right place. Unfortunately, you don't have the faintest idea what's going on, even in your own circle," Gabe said. He continued, "Someone did a study once where they gave two children a board game to play—something basically like checkers, except each player only had once piece, and the object of the game was to try to get it to the other side of the board. If the other player blocked you, you couldn't advance, and therefore, couldn't win. When someone did win, they got a piece of candy. They tried this with children all over the world, who quickly figured out that by getting out of each other's way, they could both reach the other side—they could both win. There was only one country in the entire world where the children invariably blocked each other. Just one: America. The kids would block each other, so the game ended and nobody got a treat. The sociologists doing the study thought maybe they didn't get the concept that it was possible for both of them to win, so they started making suggestions to them after a while, pointing out that if they both moved their pieces differently, the game wouldn't end in a stalemate. But you know what the kids all said?"

"What?" Bryce asked.

"They said they didn't want the other kid to win, even if it meant forfeiting their own piece of candy," Gabe explained. "That's the difference between a cooperative mentality and a competitive mentality."

"Okay," Bryce said, "So America's full of hypercompetitive children who can't conceive of a win-win outcome. What does that have to do with anything?"

"It has everything to do with it," Gabe said. "When we see everyone else as a competitor for a dwindling set of resources, we get selfish; we get stupid. We do things that harm others, and especially, we devalue others. As long as everyone we see is an 'other' to be feared and conquered, and as long as we put the wants of the individual—of *certain* individuals— above the needs of the collective, we're going to devolve rather than advance. In fact, it's a process that's well underway."

"You mean the way New Money is taking over everything and ruining it?" Bryce said.

"They're part of it," Gabe said. "But I'm talking about the people at the top, the ones who are calling all the shots."

"Wait—" Bryce said, "if you mean people from our class, I admit we've committed plenty of wrongs, but at the end of the day, we want society to do well."

At that, Gabe smiled and shook his head.

"Do you ever do any air-conducting?" he asked.

"What?" asked Bryce.

"Air-conducting. You know, waving your arms around, pretending to be conducting the orchestra when you're listening to music?"

"Oh, that; well, yes, sometimes," he admitted sheepishly.

"But you know you're not the one who's really telling those instruments what to do, right?" Gabe asked.

"Of course," Bryce said.

"Well, I'm glad you're sitting down because you and I and everyone in the world we come from have been air-conducting for a long, long time," Gabe said. "The only problem is that we believed we actually were conducting. If that were true, the *nouveau riche* never would've attained the influence they have. I mean, if we really had that much power, how could a boatload of tacky new millionaires take it all away from us?"

"So they're the ones who are really conducting?" Bryce asked.

"No. It goes even higher than that," Gabe said. He paused a moment before adding, "Bilderberg."

Bryce had never heard that name before.

"Who's Bilderberg?" he said.

Gabe laughed. "The Bilderberg Group."

"I'm not familiar with them," Bryce said.

"No one is," Gabe told him. "They hide in plain sight. You can find out practically anything about them, only nobody bothers because they aren't even aware of their existence."

"So what's the Bilderberg Group?" Bryce asked.

"It's a loose collective of high-level individuals from around the world, and they get together periodically to discuss and mobilize their plans for the future. They're just a modern extension of the Old World powers that ruled Europe for centuries. Anyway, while the Great and Powerful Oz is out there shooting his mouth off and looking tough, they're behind the curtain, pulling the levers and pushing the buttons," he said.

"I'm not following you," Bryce said, feeling like he'd just stepped off a merry-go-round.

"I'll break it down for you," Gabe said. "We come from a class with inherited wealth. We embrace a lifestyle of thrift and social conservatism, and we try to be charitable, preferably from a distance. We're overeducated, polite, and we keep a low profile. Some of us have immense wealth, but most of us are just comfortable. Relatively speaking, of course," Gabe quickly added. He went on. "Beneath us are the middle class—or what's left of them—and below that are the working people, otherwise known as dumb sheep."

"'Dumb sheep?' I wouldn't go that far," Bryce protested.

"Why not?" Gabe asked. "Jesus did. Very informative book, the Bible. Everything you could ever want to know about human nature is all there in black and white. Our Lord was a shrewd teacher, and he warned that the common people were like a flock of sheep—an easy target for the malevolent. He gave all kinds of illustrations, hoping he could show them how to tell the difference between good shepherds and people who were out to harm them, but it never really sunk in. Personally, I think Christ was counting on the brighter members of society to lead them in the right direction because at the end of the day, sheep need a shepherd. Ask any farmer. They'll die without someone to take care of them. Unfortunately, farmers aren't the only ones who know this. The corrupt among us figured it out pretty quickly and turned it to their advantage. How else do you think they were able to turn blue-collar workers from union-loving compatriots who fought for the welfare of the Common Man into a bunch of irate reactionaries who vote against their own interests and actually believe that the exorbitant salaries of corporate executives are justified because they work so much harder than they do? You have some guy working three jobs who still can't feed his family voting against social welfare programs? That's not political hokeypokey. That's black magic."

Gabe paused, but only long enough to take a breath before continuing.

"Then along come the *nouveau riche*, who haven't yet figured out that once they work the poor to death, there'll be nobody left to clean their toilets. You can't help but love them. Their biggest fear is that the pilot who flies their private jet to their secret bunker in New Zealand when society collapses will want to bring his family along. Until then, they institute as many policies as possible to keep the masses so exhausted, sick, and despondent that they'll never mount an all-out revolution. That's the stuff of their nightmares. Fortunately, they've discovered that buying solid gold Lamborghinis and 500-foot yachts goes a long way towards distracting them from imagining their own heads on a pike."

"Where is this all going?" Bryce asked.

"The short answer? Feudalism. De-industrialization. A renaissance is only allowed when the powers that be need new ideas and technological progress, then they cut everyone down again once they have what they need. Eventually, after a lot of pieces have been removed from the board, it's going to look like a game of chess featuring only kings and queens—a collection of super-rich individuals who aren't accountable to anyone, and whose power is only limited by the other kings and queens on the chessboard. The rest of us are basically going to be serfs, and what little social safety nets we had will be long gone," Gabe said.

"Don't you think that's an awfully pessimistic outlook?" Bryce said. "I mean, maybe what you're saying might be possible from a theoretical standpoint, but surely, nothing like that could ever really happen."

"You're already thirty years too late. It's happening. Right now, aquifers are being bought up at a rate that would make your head spin. Water is the next big resource that the people in control are going to seize to ensure their power."

Bryce remembered what Len Fernando had told him about outrunning his enemies. Now he understood.

"If all this is so, why should I even bother starting a nonprofit? What's the point in doing anything?" Bryce asked.

Gabe finished his wine. He set the glass down gently and looked at it as he answered.

"To be honest, I'm not sure," he said, "I know I felt like that every morning when I got up in Southie, but I did get up, and somehow everything worked out. I have to believe we've got something on our side, and I think whatever it is has to do with making them see things for what they are. John Kenneth Galbraith said that the powerful fear radicals more than anything else, but that their greatest danger is accepting their own myth. He said 'Exposure to reality remains the nemesis of the great.'"

They sat in silence for a moment, and then Totti came to clear their plates.

"I hate to ask," Bryce said, "but do you think people like us will survive?"

Gabe shrugged. "We're resilient and we have good financial habits. I don't think Old Money will ever really vanish, it'll just change form. We'll get jobs, trim our charity commitments, and cut back on travel, but let's face it, our mothers were slipcovering couches even when money wasn't tight, so as far as day-to-day life goes, I don't think we'll notice much of a difference."

Bryce felt a little better hearing that. He wondered what time it was and remembered his watch was out for repair.

"Do you have the time?" he asked Gabe.

"No, I'm afraid I don't wear a timepiece during social engagements," he said.

Bryce felt his face reddening for having shown such bad manners. Bryce had been raised as a gentleman, but the exchange proved that Gabe hailed from a far loftier upbringing, in which the company of the person one was with was so important that concerns about the passing of time were considered crass and disrespectful.

After the check was paid, they briefly discussed possible strategies for Bryce's nonprofit and promised to get together again. Bryce had come to the conclusion that Gabe was a remarkable person indeed, and he felt like he could learn much from him.

On the way out, Bryce said, "By the way, I have to ask, what's that cologne you're wearing?"

"Old Spice."

21

Bryce had to admit that he was surprised to hear from Rosemary that night. She'd been off mooning after her priest and had barely even bothered to monitor Bryce's spiritual progress.

"So much for helping me see the light," he joked.

"You know I didn't mean to seem disinterested. I've just had a lot going on. Tell me what your latest insights have been," she asked.

"At lunch today, I discussed Biblical allusions to sheep," he said. "At great length, I might add."

Rosemary giggled.

"What was that about?" she asked.

"It was part of a conversation about socioeconomics," he explained.

"You mean how the working class are just dumb sheep?" she said.

"You're familiar with this concept?" he asked.

She said, "Bryce, it's old news. Catch up."

"I bet you've never heard of the Bilderberg Group," he taunted.

"Then you'd be wrong. They started at the Bilderberg Hotel in the Netherlands in 1954. They have ties to the most powerful individuals and institutions on the planet. Sorry to disappoint you," she said, "but nothing slips past me."

"In that case," Bryce said, "You're even more amazing than I thought."

"Who the hell were you having lunch with?" she asked.

“An interesting friend of Patty’s who’s lived at both ends of the social spectrum. He’s a hybrid. Pretty remarkable guy. We talked about a lot of things,” Bryce said.

“Speaking of,” she asked, “what’s going on with Patty and Susan?”

“No change as far as I know,” Bryce said. “I’m just hoping Patty comes to her senses.”

“How’s Susan?” Rosemary asked.

“This has been really difficult for her,” he said. “She’s doing everything she can, but Patty’s probably going to win custody.”

“That’s such a shame,” Rosemary said. “By the way, have you heard from Topher lately?”

“No,” Bryce said. “In fact, I don’t think I’ve talked to him since the workshop.”

“We spoke yesterday. His ex-wife lost the baby,” she said.

“Stephanie lost the baby?” Bryce said.

“Yes. He said it was especially terrible because she was pretty far along. The doctor said the baby’s heart stopped beating. They had to induce labor,” she said.

“Is she okay?” Bryce asked.

“She’ll be fine but Topher said this has destroyed her emotionally.”

“Well, she’s covered there,” Bryce said. “Her boyfriend, Ambrose, is a therapist.”

“Ambrose is gone,” said Rosemary. “Topher said he walked out on her right after she was discharged from the hospital.”

“How could he?” exclaimed Bryce.

“I don’t know,” Rosemary said. “Maybe the baby was the only reason he was staying.”

Bryce reflected that a therapist who slept with his patients didn’t exactly live by a sterling moral code, so he concluded he shouldn’t have been surprised.

“At least she’s got Topher,” Rosemary said. “He’s been looking after her.”

“Do you think they’ll get back together?” he asked.

“Nah,” Rosemary said. “He and Juliette are pretty tight. He’s got his own life now, but he still cares about her. She’s lucky to have him around.”

By the time Bryce finished dinner shortly afterwards, his head was reeling. Between his discussion with Gabe and finding out about Stephanie’s situation, he felt a sense of agitation, but it was more of a call to action than restless anxiety.

It wasn’t yet 6PM, but it was dark, so he went to bed. He had a cup of cocoa and went to sleep.

22

The next morning as Bryce waited for Stephanie to answer the phone, he contemplated what a terrible time of year it was for a tragedy. Christmas was just a month away. He hoped she wouldn't be reminded of her loss every holiday season from now on.

When she answered, Bryce could tell she'd been crying. Either that, or she'd suddenly developed a raging head cold. He had an idea to offer her to stay at the cabin for a while as a sort of getaway, since he reasoned she probably didn't feel well enough to take a formal vacation. He could stay at Susan's. It would give her a chance to enjoy some tranquility in the country, but she said she felt more comfortable convalescing at home. However, she said she would like to see him and asked if she could come up some time.

"Any time you like," he said. "Are you sure you don't want me to come down there to visit you?"

"No," she said. "I'd rather meet you there. Would tonight be too short notice?" she asked.

It wasn't like Stephanie to make spontaneous social engagements, but he agreed. She said she had a follow-up visit with her doctor and then she'd need some rest, but she'd be there for an early dinner. Bryce said he'd cook for them so they didn't have to go out in public. She said she appreciated that.

That night, while he waited for her to arrive, he opened a bottle of wine and thought about all the years they'd known each other since childhood in Ardsley. She was a lovely woman, and he realized his life would've been profoundly normal had they married after college. Sometimes he wished they had, just for the sake of having that normal of a life.

When he opened the door for her, Bryce saw that Stephanie looked very tired, but she appeared glad to see him. She was a bit heavier than the last time he had seen her, and she was wearing a giant wool poncho to cover her form, which still hadn't returned to normal.

He invited her to sit down and offered her a glass of wine.

"No," she said, "I shouldn't. They've got me on a lot of different medications."

He brought her some ginger ale instead.

They sat by the fire and chatted a little about the incident itself, and how heartbreaking it was for her to learn of her child's death and then have to deliver it, only to know it was going to be placed into a coffin rather than a cradle. It had been a boy. She talked about her sadness at Ambrose's departure, which was as brief as it was swift. He had given her life a needed measure of stability, which is why she was grateful for Topher's continued devotion during her time of sorrow, and for their friendship, which had outlived their marriage.

Finally, she said, "You're probably wondering why I'm here. There's something I need to tell you, Bryce. The baby was yours."

Bryce said nothing. He was utterly astonished.

"When we were together, I forgot about birth control because Topher couldn't have children, so I just wasn't used to using it. I didn't think I'd get pregnant," she explained, "And I didn't tell you until now because I didn't want you to feel that you had any obligation to me or to the baby. I knew you didn't want our relationship to continue. But now, it makes no difference. You might as well know the truth."

When he could finally speak, Bryce said, "How do you know it wasn't Ambrose's baby?"

"I didn't sleep with him until about a month after you and I broke up," she said. "I'd already had a pregnancy test by then."

"Did Ambrose know?" Bryce asked.

"I didn't tell him at the time," she said. "He only found out because of this, when he overheard the doctor say I was due in January. I'd been fudging the dates whenever we talked about it."

"So all that while, he thought it was his," Bryce said.

"I felt so bad when I saw how upset he was that we lost the baby. I was kind of glad when he found out, even though I hadn't intended for that to happen," she said.

"Was he angry at you?" Bryce asked.

Stephanie shook her head. "We didn't really talk about it, and then he left and didn't answer my call when I contacted him afterwards. My mother drove me home, and when I got there, I saw that he'd taken a few of his things and left. I haven't heard from him since."

Bryce's thoughts turned to his own place in the scheme of things, now that he had begun to take it all in.

"Do you need anything from me?" he asked.

"Nothing," she said. "I just wanted you to know."

"You wanted me to know that if this hadn't happened, another man would be raising my child?" Bryce said.

Stephanie started to cry.

"I'm sorry," she said, "My emotions have been all over the place. I didn't mean to hurt you. I thought I was doing the best thing possible for everyone concerned."

Bryce held her as she cried on his shoulder.

"Oh Bryce," she said, "It was the happiest I've ever been, thinking I was going to have our baby, and now this."

"It's okay," he said. "It's all going to be okay."

When she stopped crying, he dabbed her face with his handkerchief. Her eyes were swollen and she looked terrible, but he knew she would cope with everything.

"I feel so foolish," she said. "Running off with my therapist. God, who does that?"

"We all do a lot of foolish things," he said. "Why don't we have dinner?"

"I'm not very hungry," she said.

"I know, but at least have a little. I made Chicken à la King over toast, your favorite," Bryce said.

"Really? You did that for me?" she said.

"Of course. You know I care about you. I only want you to be happy," he said. "Come on, please come to the table. Eating will make you feel better."

She didn't stay long, but they did have a nice time. While they ate, they talked about old times back in Ardsley and how long ago those days seemed to them now.

When she left, she kissed him goodbye and he said he'd touch base with her in a few days to see how she was doing.

Bryce heard her car engine start and then the sound of it as it vanished down the driveway.

He went and sat in Grandfather's old chair and stared into the fire. He could barely process everything he was thinking. Unbeknownst to him, he had fathered a child which would've been raised by his longtime friend, with whom he'd had an illicit affair, and by a Canadian therapist who'd been led to believe the baby was his own.

So much had happened of which he was directly involved but wholly ignorant. It was troublesome to think of it all now, knowing his child was lying in a cemetery somewhere.

What did she name him? Bryce suddenly wondered. He'd forgotten to ask.

23

"There wasn't anything you could've done, Bryce, you know that," Deek said. "You didn't even know about it until a week ago."

Deek, Tiffany, and Bryce were attending a fundraiser to benefit a Jewish community health center. Tiffany had heard about it somewhere and decided she wanted to make a large contribution, and she also wanted an invitation to the event, so Deek made it happen. He was good at doing that.

They were having cocktails and discussing Bryce's news about Stephanie and the baby. Bryce said he felt he'd let her down somehow, but they assured him he was an innocent bystander.

"You can't do nothing—I mean, anything—about it if you don't know about it," Tiffany told him.

An older woman with short salt-and-pepper hair and a sequined blouse approached them and came up to Tiffany, reading her name tag.

"Tiffany, I thought that was you," she said, giving her a light hug. "I have a knack for being able to tell who's who. I'm Chick Schatz. I wanted to thank you personally for your generosity. We truly appreciate it. And this must be your charming fiancé," she said, turning to Deek.

"Yes, Ma'am," he said. "That would be me."

"Such a lovely young couple," she said, smiling. "And who's this character?" she asked, putting her hand on Bryce's arm.

"I'm Bryce Parnell, a friend," he said, shaking her hand. "How do you do?"

"Are you all having a good time?" she asked.

"Yes," said Tiffany. "I've never been to anything Jewish before, but I heard the health center helps a lot of people and I wanted to donate some money."

"Aren't you kind?" Chick said joyfully. "That means a lot to us, it really does. You see, in my religion, we believe it's important to look out for others. The concept of social justice is nothing new to us. That's because we know we're all connected. Every one of us. And so when our children are little, we give them a tzedakah box, which is a container to save money for charity. It can be a little box or a can or anything, and maybe they decorate it on the outside, and then before Shabbat every week—that's our special holy time that starts on Friday night—the children put money into it. When the box gets full, they give the money to someone in need."

"That's a beautiful tradition," said Bryce.

"Yes, so you see, my dear," said Chick, addressing Tiffany, "you are a shining example of what happens when we give from the heart."

"I just wanted to do something good for you," Tiffany said, shrugging.

"That's all it takes. In fact, if you're interested, I could find out about getting you involved, maybe on the board?" Chick said.

"I don't want to do anything like that," Tiffany said, "but for a party like this, there's a lot of decorations to put up and take down. If you ever have another one, I could help, I mean, if I'm allowed. I like decorating."

"Would you listen to this? 'If I'm allowed,'" Chick jokingly mimicked. "Trust me, there will be many, many more parties like this and we would be thrilled to have your help. I'll talk Mimi. She chairs the Events Committee. You'll be hearing from her."

Bryce and Deek glanced at each other over Tiffany's head. Chick thanked Tiffany again and went off to mingle with the other attendees.

"That's so cool that they have a special charity box," Tiffany said. "I like Chick." Then she added, "Do you think they let people become Jewish?"

"Let's take things one step at a time," Deek said. "You've already changed a lot in the past few months."

Bryce said, “I’m sure they’d let you, but religious conversion is the kind of thing you should consider carefully.”

“Oh I know,” said Tiffany. “I just mean I like what they believe, about everyone being connected and looking out for other people. That should be everyone’s religion.”

“I think that’s the most profound thing you’ve ever said,” Bryce told her.

“I’m really proud of you,” Deek said to Tiffany. “See? I told you you’d get the hang of this lifestyle eventually.”

“Well, as long as I can do it my own way,” she said.

Just then, she reached out and grabbed the wall next to her for support. Deek put his hands on her to steady her. She was staring straight ahead, but she looked like she was going to faint.

“What is it? Are you okay?” Bryce asked.

“Bryce,” she said, “I just had a vision. It was about you.”

“Let’s get you to a chair,” Deek said.

“No!” Tiffany exclaimed. “Let me finish. It was about rain. There was so much rain.”

“You saw me in the rain?” Bryce asked.

“Yeah, but there was more. It’s something big,” she said. “I can’t see it, but I can feel it.”

“What does it feel like?” Bryce asked.

“It hurts very much. It hurts—it hurts so much,” she said. “Bryce, you gotta be prepared. It’s gonna be bad.”

“But we don’t know what it is,” he said.

Tiffany looked shaken. She took a few deep breaths and quickly excused herself to the ladies’ room.

“What do you think that was about?” Bryce asked.

“I don’t know, but I wouldn’t doubt her,” Deek said. “You know she’s been right about you before. She said there are some people she gets a stronger signal on, and you’re one of them.”

“It probably means I’ll have a hole in my new roof,” Bryce joked. “I already spent a fortune on it. I hardly want to go through that again.”

The rest of the evening passed pleasantly and Bryce returned home to find Suki on his doorstep. He called the Fentons, who came in their big red truck to get her. He thought about making a comical remark about her being a Chocolate Lab, but relations between them had recently become cordial again and he didn’t want to risk it.

24

Christmas was drawing nigh, and Bryce and Aunt Bitsy made their annual pilgrimage to the theatre. They'd had lunch at one of Aunt Bitsy's favorite old establishments in the city, but she lamented that they no longer had Duck à L'Orange on the menu.

"Nobody serves it any more," she'd complained. "It used to be everywhere and now it's disappeared. I tell you, it's impossible to find *cuisine bourgeoise* in restaurants today."

"You don't have to convince me, Aunt Bitsy," Bryce had said. "I'm with you on that."

The show had been awful, but Bryce was expecting that. What he wasn't expecting was Aunt Bitsy's offer of a late tea once he brought her back to her house in New Rochelle. Clearly, she wanted to talk about something.

"Bryce," she said, as her maid Essie served them tea and cookies, "I'm quite concerned about Susan. This mess with Patty is taking a terrible toll on her. I don't believe she's getting enough rest."

"Probably not," Bryce said, reaching for a gingersnap. "I can try convincing her to take a break, but you know Susan."

"That's along the lines of what I was thinking. She loves the cabin. It reminds her of your Grandfather Parnell. Why not have her up there for a weekend? Maybe take her out to a concert or something to get her mind off things," she suggested.

"That's a good idea, but ultimately, either she will or she won't. I can only offer," he said.

"Of course, dear, that's all any of us can do. And how are things with Rosemary?" she asked, changing the subject.

"I'm not sure," Bryce said. "She's still involved with that priest."

"Yes," Aunt Bitsy said in a tone of voice that subtly conveyed a surge of disapproval. "And what about Stephanie? Is she still mixed up with that head-shrinker?"

Bryce had to stifle a laugh. "No, Ambrose left her." Then, turning serious, he said, "She lost the baby."

"Oh my," Aunt Bitsy said, "But I am sorry to hear that. That's just dreadful, even if she did cuckhold her husband. Nobody deserves that. Losing a child is the hardest thing in the world."

Aunt Bitsy's daughter had been killed in a car crash out on Long Island one summer when Bryce was little. He knew she spoke from experience.

"When my Pamela died, it was as if the world ended. Losing anyone is terrible, but especially under such tragic circumstances," she said.

"It was a drunk driver, wasn't it?" Bryce asked.

Aunt Bitsy looked down into her cup before she answered.

"There's more to the story than you know," she said, looking up at Bryce with a pained expression. "That summer, we were renting a cottage and Pamela got mixed up with some boy, some local boy in the town. I think he pumped gasoline or something. His family weren't summer people, they lived there year-round. She'd been seeing him, and Edward and I thought they were getting too familiar, so we told her that anything beyond a casual friendship was unacceptable. She was just at that age where they start to believe they know better than everyone, and I think her pride was wounded. She told us that they were in love. Looking back, if I could relive those moments, I'd have let her do anything she wanted, but of course, we couldn't do that, Edward and I, and we had quite a heated row about it. She told us that this boy had proposed and that they were going to run away and get married."

"I had no idea," Bryce said.

"You were little at the time, and even years later, your mother wasn't the type to talk about such things," Aunt Bitsy said. "Anyway, as you can imagine, I was upset about the situation, but Edward was incensed. He told her that if they got married, he would have it annulled. At that point, Pamela said that if they couldn't be together, life wasn't worth living. She drove off and we assumed it had just been an expression—a turn of phrase—to indicate how very angry she was."

At that point, Aunt Bitsy discreetly wiped a tear out of the corner of her eye. She collected herself and finished the story.

"We debated about whether or not to go out and try finding her, but it wasn't long before the sheriff called. Pamela had driven at high speed into a tree, three miles from the cottage. She was killed instantly, he told us. She didn't suffer."

"I'm so sorry; I never knew," Bryce said. He could tell she clung to the sheriff's words about Pamela not suffering.

"Your mother was so good to me during that dark time," Aunt Bitsy said. "I'll never forget her kindness. Never. She was a true friend. That's why you and Susan mean the world to me. Filling her role is the least I can do for everything she did for me. Please promise me you'll look after Susan. Now, of all times, she needs a brother's love."

"I will, Aunt Bitsy," he promised.

They finished their tea, and after Essie saw him out a while later, he reflected on the sad irony that he and Aunt Bitsy shared a common grief, even though he knew he could never tell her about the loss of his son.

25

The following Sunday, he was preparing to head off to Tuxedo Park to see Susan. They were going to spend the afternoon together. He'd invited her up to the cabin, but she said she preferred to remain at home in case there were any legal developments. The study was her war room, and she didn't want to be far from it.

When he'd called her the previous week to make their plans, they'd talked for a while. Susan vented about Patty to the point that Bryce really felt that changing the subject would be better than letting her continue. She was only upsetting herself. She was obviously fearful she'd never see the baby again, and frustrated by Seth's inability to overcome the legal obstacles the Robinsons had constructed.

"Did I tell you that Gabe and I are planning to have lunch again?" Bryce had said.

"Let me guess, you two are planning the overthrow of the evil capitalist regime," she'd quipped.

"No, just some ideas for getting major donors interested in my charity. Oh, and speaking of charity," Bryce had said, "Tiffany has become a philanthropist. She also wants to convert to Judaism."

"At least she's not getting thrown out of restaurants any more," Susan had said. "By the way, I heard that Stephanie's no longer with that therapist of hers. Did you know about that?"

"Yes," Bryce had told her. "I saw her a few weeks ago. She lost the baby, but she's coping as well as can be expected."

Susan was sorry to hear the news since she'd only been informed of Ambrose's departure.

Bryce didn't want her dwelling on anything unpleasant, so he'd ended the conversation there.

After they'd spoken, he'd decided to do whatever he could to make his upcoming visit special. Over the ensuing days leading up to the weekend, he bought her a huge bottle of her favorite imported bath salts and several Rigaud candles, which he knew she'd enjoy. He'd also ordered her a carrot cake—her favorite—from a local bakery. Maybe he couldn't remedy the situation she was in, but he was going to try his best to make her more comfortable while she endured it.

After he showered and dressed, Bryce remembered she'd asked him to bring some of grandfather's genealogical charts to her. His files were still in the cabin. Bryce had forgotten exactly which ones she wanted. He gave her a quick call.

After she'd enumerated the desired documents, she said, "Before I forget, Father Jeff said to say hello to you."

"You were at Mass today?" he asked. Susan wasn't a devout churchgoer, but she did go many times a year—certainly enough not to have the church staff classify her as a "C and E Only," meaning those who only set foot in the building for Christmas and Easter.

"It was a nice service. Father Jeff had some insightful things to say," Susan said.

"I'm glad to hear you got something out of it," he said.

"Well, it's only fair considering he got something out of me: sixty dollars in the collection plate, to be precise" she said.

Bryce laughed. He was glad to hear that she was in good spirits and that whatever Father Jeff had preached about had given her good things to think about. Bryce was really starting to believe that there was more to religion than he had previously acknowledged.

"He has a way of putting things in perspective. I'm having Alexandra's nursery repainted and I'm going to fix it up so it'll be lovely when she visits. I have to keep believing that I'll get visitation eventually, even if not at first," she said.

"That's the attitude," he said. "When Stephanie and I were talking, she said she copes with her troubles by focusing on what she can do. She's thinking of joining the gardening club."

"I still don't understand why you threw her over for Cristina. Stephanie was head over heels for you," Susan said.

"She's probably the only woman in the world who's ever felt that way about me," Bryce laughed.

"Well, now's your chance," Susan said cheerfully. "Mother always did hope that the two of you would get married someday."

"Mother married into the Parnell family. I think that speaks volumes about her marital judgment," Bryce said, adding, "I have an errand to do before I get on the road, so I'd better be going."

"Okay," Susan said. "See you soon."

Bryce packed up Susan's presents and drove into town, stopping off at the bakery, where he picked up her carrot cake. During the journey to Susan's, he glanced over at the genealogy files, which were in a folder on the front seat. The information they contained detailed Bryce's heritage going back several centuries. From the hundreds of people that had contributed to his existence, the only Parnells left were Uncle Clement, Susan, and himself. Sandy was the candidate for the new generation, but Bryce worried that Patty might raise her without any understanding of that side of her family, which he felt would be a shame. With any luck, things would turn around for Patty and Susan. At least Bryce hoped they would. If Susan's mood today were any indication, maybe there was a chance.

When Bryce arrived at Tuxedo Park, he pulled through the guard house after being admitted. He drove the familiar streets until he was met with an unexpected sight. There seemed to be some kind of commotion up ahead near Susan's house. He hoped nothing was wrong over at Nathalie and Ben's. Bryce could make out a fire truck and police car, and as he drew nearer, he saw an ambulance in Susan's driveway and another unfamiliar vehicle.

Maybe something happened to Margaret, he thought.

He pulled to one side of the road and got out. A policeman came out the front door, followed by another man, and then two men that looked like emergency medical technicians. Bryce crossed the street to Susan's. He hoped whatever had happened to Margaret hadn't been serious. Probably just a bad cut while she was chopping vegetables, or maybe she'd scalded herself while boiling tea. Whatever it was, obviously Susan had called in the cavalry to look after her. Susan always knew how to take care of others.

As Bryce came up the walkway, the policeman approached him.

"This is my sister's house. I'm Bryce Parnell," he said. He realized his voice was shaking. There, standing at the front door, was Margaret. She held her fingertips over her mouth and looked like she was in a state of distress.

"I'm sorry for your loss, sir," the officer said.

"What loss?" Bryce asked. He was trembling.

"Oh, I thought you'd been informed. Your sister—"

Bryce didn't hear what followed because he couldn't take his eyes off the stretcher that was emerging from the doorway. It bore a physical form, covered with a sheet.

"Susan?" he said, his blood turning to ice.

He ran to the stretcher, but someone guided him back towards the house. He heard Margaret saying something that didn't register. She was upset. Very upset. Then Nathalie came out of the house, then Ben. Everyone was talking and he couldn't understand anything anyone was saying. All of a sudden, colored lights were flashing everywhere as the emergency vehicles started up. There was a deafening roar of engines, and then they drove away.

In the quiet that followed their departure, Bryce stood on the lawn, looking after them even though they were gone. They had taken his sister away.

He felt a warm hand holding his. It was Nathalie. She led him into the house.

Bryce felt his heart pounding so hard he though it would come straight out of his chest. Someone helped him off with his coat and sat him down on the couch. Ben handed him a glass of water and made him drink it. Then he sat down next to him. He didn't say anything, but he put his hand on Bryce's shoulder and kept it there. To Bryce, it felt like a lifeline, a reminder that there was something outside of him helping to keep him from shattering into a million tiny pieces.

Margaret and Nathalie came into the sitting room.

"Please sit down, Margaret," Nathalie was saying. "I've got the tea."

Margaret was wringing her hands. When she finally made eye contact with Bryce, she started to cry.

"I'm so sorry," she said. "It was such a shock—such a shock. I did everything I could."

"What happened?" Bryce asked. His brain was finally starting to engage.

Margaret wiped her face with a tissue and took a deep breath.

"Shortly after you called, her lawyer, Seth, telephoned here. He'd just spoken with one of Ms. Robinson's lawyers and it was very bad news. I heard Ms. Parnell shouting in the study, getting very worked up. When she came out, she told me all about it. I didn't really follow, but it was something to do with not getting custody of the baby."

At this point, Margaret made a sniffling sound and caught her breath, but then she continued.

"She'd been in such a good mood all morning, it was terrible to see her so agitated. I told her I'd make some chamomile tea to calm her down and she said she would like that, so I went into the kitchen and a few minutes later, when I came out with the tea, she was sitting there on the couch, all slumped down, with her chin on her chest. Well, I rushed over and felt for a pulse but there was nothing, so I called 911 and they came right over. Heart attack, the coroner said." Then Margaret started wailing. "Poor Ms. Parnell!"

Nathalie comforted her.

"But she can't be gone," Bryce said. "I was just talking to her."

"When was that?" asked Ben.

"Right before I came here. I gave her a call, and then I went to the bakery to pick up her carrot cake," Bryce said.

"It's a long way from Connecticut," Ben explained. "It happened a long time before you got here."

Just then, Ingrid Masterson, Nathalie's mother, let herself in.

"Oh Bryce," she said. "I'm so glad you're here. Very sad about Susan. But don't you worry about anything. We'll look after you." She turned to Margaret. "John is on his way. He'll be staying with you here tonight."

"I can put up a stew," Margaret said. "My John loves stew." She headed for the kitchen.

"I'll help you," Ben said. "I love to cook."

"What about the other call?" Nathalie asked quietly, once they'd left the room.

Ingrid nodded. "I told her."

"You mean Patty?" Bryce asked.

"Yes," Ingrid said.

"How did she take it?" he asked.

"She was distraught," Ingrid said. "Practically hysterical."

Bryce couldn't imagine Patty's reaction to the news. In his mind, she had been the cause of his sister's death, with her dramatic backlash to a handful of perceived slights and a childish disagreement about hiring extra staff. Her vindictiveness had escalated his sister's stress to fatal levels.

"Bryce," Nathalie asked, "Didn't you say you had a cake in the car? Let me have your keys. I'll bring it into the house."

"I can do that," Ingrid said, taking his keys and going out the front door.

Nathalie sat next to him and held his hand.

"The cake's for Susan," Bryce said. "All the way here in the car, I kept the box very still. I was really careful not to smudge the frosting. That's Susan's favorite part."

Before he knew what was happening, Nathalie was saying "It's all right," and he was crying.

"I was just talking with her," he sobbed over and over.

"Susan is dead, Bryce," Nathalie said. "But you're okay. Everything's going to be okay."

When Ingrid returned, she poured Bryce a shot of whiskey.

"Drink this straight down," she said, handing it to him. He drank it, and soon he felt a warmth in his chest that was relaxing and slightly numbing. It was a relief to feel that way.

There was a knock at the door. Ingrid answered it.

"Bryce, I came over as soon as I heard," Father Jeff was saying. "I'm sure you don't want me disturbing you at a time like this, but I wanted to offer my condolences and let you know that I'm here if you need me. Any time, day or night."

"Thank you," Bryce said.

"We all loved Susan very much. She was a good woman. I'm truly sorry, Bryce," Father Jeff said.

"What time should we come by tomorrow?" Ingrid asked.

"I'm here whenever you are," he said. She saw him out.

Bryce felt like he was waiting for a bus, but as far as he knew, he wasn't waiting for anything. In fact, he felt like he wanted to get away from something, but he wasn't sure what. He had a vague feeling that there were a lot of things he was going to have to think about, but he didn't have the energy. Ingrid must have read his thoughts.

"Bryce, tomorrow we'll meet with Father Jeff to discuss the funeral, so don't worry about that, and we'll help you with the reception," she said slowly. She knew it was a lot for him to take in, so she was making it easy. "John is coming to stay with Margaret tonight, but eventually you'll have to decide if you want her to stay on here or not. I recommend giving her a few weeks off so everyone has time to collect their thoughts. In the meantime, I can have Polly take care of whatever needs seeing to over here. As far as notifications, I'll call your Uncle Clement later unless you'd rather tell him yourself. We must also be mindful of his age and make sure someone's there, that he's not alone when we tell him. It's apt to come as quite a shock."

Bryce forgot about Uncle Clement.

"As for you," Ingrid said, "Are there any friends of yours you'd like me to call?"

Bryce shook his head. "I can do it," he said.

"Okay," said Ingrid, "But if you change your mind, let me know. It can get to be a bit much. Now about tonight, where will you be staying? I think driving back to Norfolk's out of the question. You can stay here, but we'd love it if you came and spent the night at our house. You'll be more comfortable and Polly can look after you. If you stay here, it's not really fair to Margaret."

Bryce had a feeling Ingrid was right. He couldn't expect Margaret to continue with her duties after what she'd been through.

"I'll stay at your place, then, but I don't think I'll be very good company," Bryce said.

"That's quite all right," Ingrid said with a smile. "You just be yourself."

"Thank you, Ingrid," he said. "I really appreciate everything."

"Susan was a huge help when Minty died. We're merely returning the favor," she said. "I'm only sorry it has to be this way. I never imagined anything like this."

"Neither did I," Bryce said.

Ingrid hesitated a moment and then said, "Now there's one last thing, and that's legal matters. Susan's lawyer will have to be informed, and I think we should do so immediately. He's going to have a lot on his plate between dealing with her will as well as the pending legal issues. I don't have his phone number, but it's probably in Susan's study. Would you like me to call him?"

"No," said Bryce as he stood up, "I'll call him."

As Bryce walked down the hallway to the study, he remembered that a death was never real to you until you had to tell someone else about it, at least that was how it had felt with his father, his mother, and Grandfather. He wasn't looking forward to the task, but he knew it had to be done.

Sitting at Susan's desk, he flipped through her phone directory, picked up the receiver, and dialed a number. When the man on the other end of the line answered, he told him who he was.

"Hello, Bryce," Seth said. "What can I do for you?"

"I'm afraid I'm calling with bad news. My sister passed away this afternoon," he said. The words rang in his ears.

There was shocked silence from the other end, and then Seth said, "I'm terribly sorry for your loss. Susan was a wonderful person."

"Yes, she was. She had a heart attack shortly after her last conversation with you," Bryce said. "Apparently, she was very distressed."

"We were discussing some disturbing new developments in her custody case. She was very upset about it," he said.

"Yes, I'm sure she was. At any rate, I don't know what this does to her legal situation and frankly, I really don't think I'm in any shape to discuss it right now, but please get back to me later this week and we can discuss everything," Bryce said, giving Seth his phone number.

"Thank you for informing me, Bryce," Seth said. "And please know that I'll be keeping your family in my thoughts and prayers."

Bryce hung up the phone and sighed deeply. It was done.

When he came out of the study, John was waiting for him.

"I got here as quick as I could," he said. "I'm really sorry about your sister."

"Thank you," Bryce said.

"Listen, my mother's not doing too well, so I'll be sticking around tonight if that's okay, but I wanted to let you know that I'll be covering for her. Please, don't hesitate to call me if you want tea or some food. I can definitely manage."

"That's very kind of you, John," Bryce said. "Actually, I'll be heading over to the Masterson's soon. In the meantime, if anything comes up, just call me over there, and of course, if Mrs. Masterson asks you to do anything, you have my approval."

"Very good," John said nodding. "Will do."

Bryce felt much better knowing that John was around. He was worried about Margaret, though. She'd had a bad shock. Then he had a thought.

"John," he called out.

"Yes?" John asked, coming back down the hallway.

"For what it's worth, you and your mother can help yourself to anything in the liquor cabinet," Bryce said. "It's been a rough day."

"Thank you," John said. "That's very nice of you."

Bryce rejoined Ingrid and Nathalie. Ben returned from the kitchen now that John was there to attend to his mother.

Moments later, Bryce went next door with the Mastersons, who were very gracious to him. He wasn't hungry for dinner, but was starving an hour later. He complained of feeling a chill, and then when they turned up the heat, he was sweltering. Everyone thought he might want to rest, but for some odd reason, he wanted to watch mindless TV. Ben flipped channels, asking Bryce what he'd like to see.

When he got to a game show featuring a lot of people screaming and jumping around the stage, clapping their hands, he told Ben that was the channel he wanted. Ben sat with him the whole time. Other shows came on, but Bryce couldn't remember any of them. Around 2AM, he finally announced that he was tired, and Ben showed him up to his room.

"Thanks, Ben," Bryce said. "I owe you."

Ben simply patted him on the shoulder, and then Bryce headed to bed. For a brief while after he turned out the lights, he felt terribly alone, but then he fell into a deep sleep of absolute exhaustion.

26

When Bryce awoke, he felt well-rested but groggy. His mind wandered. He remembered a warm summer afternoon in his childhood when he and Susan had played Hide and Seek in the woods outside Grandfather's cabin. Rolling over in bed, he noticed that the sheets weren't his. He was somewhere else. He was at the Masterson's. Susan was dead.

All at once, the anguish of the previous day's events came flooding back into his mind. He was so unprepared for the pain, it took his breath away. He started to cry.

When he came down to breakfast, the family were very hospitable. Polly served him some scrambled eggs and toast, which he ate without thinking. Ingrid told him a story about an eccentric couple she met on one of her recent cruises. Nathalie and Ben said something about plans to buy a second home. It was clear they were all trying to create the illusion of normalcy, and Bryce was glad because he felt as though he'd just been hit by a truck.

Later, Ingrid and Nathalie went with him to the church to discuss the funeral with Father Jeff, while Ben attended to some business matters.

Bryce didn't have any preferences about anything, so Ingrid and Nathalie chose for him. It occurred to him that death created an awful lot of work, a fact from which he had been shielded since it was Susan who took care of their parents' deaths as well as Grandfather's. Now he understood how much she had done. He wiped away a tear that had started rolling down his cheek.

Next, they visited the funeral home and the florist, where more arrangements were to be made. He was doing fine until he had to choose a banner for his floral wreath. When he said the words "Beloved Sister" out loud, his voice broke and he unexpectedly started to cry. The florist taking their order was very kind and said that she understood.

They returned to the Masterson's for lunch, and Nathalie, who'd popped over to the house, reported that there had been a steady stream of flowers and baked goods from the neighbors.

"John certainly has his hands full. Everyone has been so thoughtful. There were flowers from the Gwynns, the Johnsons, and Mrs. Van Skoik. Linda Davis brought a plate of brownies and some handmade cards her little boys had drawn just for Susan. Isn't that sweet? And Mrs. Baraldi—the one who lives in the grey house—brought a lemon bundt cake. There were lots of other things," Nathalie said, "But I didn't take the time to look at everything."

"How's Margaret?" Bryce asked.

"Much better today," Nathalie said. "I told John you might be by this afternoon to discuss the reception and talk about the future. I hope that's okay."

"Yes," said Bryce, taking a spoonful of his broth. "It's probably best to do that as soon as possible."

"Do you have any idea of what you'd like to do?" Ingrid asked gently.

"No," Bryce said.

"There are a few options," Ingrid said. "You could move here and keep the cabin as a second residence, or you could continue living in the cabin and keep the house as an alternative home. We'd be happy to keep an eye on the place for you. And of course, you could always sell it."

"I hate to lose Margaret," Bryce said.

"Mother and I have discussed it," Nathalie said, "And if you decide to let Margaret go, we'll be happy to take her. Ben and I host a lot of large gatherings and Susan used to lend her to us, so having her here all the time would be helpful, especially after Ben and I start a family. Then again, she may want to retire, but if not, she'll always have a place with us."

"That's good," Bryce said. "I'll see what Margaret has to say."

He had a short lie-down after lunch.

What am I going to do with the house? he thought, as he stared at the ceiling.

Selling it was out of the question since it had been his mother's childhood home, but as much as he liked Tuxedo Park, he didn't want to live there. He decided to keep the house as an alternative residence, which meant Margaret wouldn't be needed. The only other option was to have her come and work for him in the cabin, but the place was far too small, and he doubted she'd want to live out in the sticks. Besides, if he gave her to the Mastersons, there was always the possibility he could re-hire her someday if needed, that is, if she didn't want to retire. Either way, it seemed like the best all-around solution.

When Bryce returned to the house a short while later to float the idea to Margaret, he noticed that a black beribboned mourning wreath had been put in place of the Christmas wreath on the front door. This would alert any callers to the fact that there had been a death in the family and to leave them in peace. Its last use had been after Grandfather's death.

When Bryce spoke with Margaret, she was receptive to work at the Masterson's.

"I hate to leave the family," she said. "I've been here since before your mother passed, God rest her soul."

"God rest her soul," John echoed, in keeping with the Irish custom.

"But Mrs. Masterson and Mrs. Lu have always been very good to me, and I suppose I can get used to that terrible dishwashing liquid that Polly uses, so I think I'd be happy working there," Margaret said.

Bryce was surprised to hear about the dishwashing soap. It occurred to him that servants probably had all kinds of things going on of which he was unaware. Theirs was such a hidden life, he reflected.

At that point, John coughed and looked like he wanted to say something.

"Yes?" Bryce said.

"I hate to bring this up at a time like this, but I have to enroll for next semester pretty soon, and I was wondering . . . " He stopped and Bryce was puzzled. What did John's college enrollment have to do with him?

Then he remembered that Susan was paying half his tuition.

"Oh that," Bryce said. "Don't worry. Whatever arrangement you had in place with Susan will continue. I'll see to it."

"Thank you," John said. "I—I wasn't sure, you know."

Bryce's mother had told him that being fair with the servants was very important. She explained that they really counted on their pay since it was all they had to live on, so being clear about arrangements, keeping promises, and paying on time were paramount. She said you could always tell the newly rich because they neglected to pay their staff on time, sometimes made assurances to cover expenses upon which they later reneged, and she'd even heard of a few cases where a maid was told to hold a check for a week or two so that it would clear. Bryce was proud the Parnells weren't like that.

Before he left, he told Margaret and John that they were welcome to stay in the house until whatever date she would begin work at the Masterson's. He would also give her severance pay. He told her the only things he expected of her until then were fielding the well-wishers who came to the door and serving at the reception, which would be held on Thursday. Ingrid would coordinate everything and Polly would help Margaret.

After that, Bryce returned to the Masterson's and Nathalie helped him compose the obituary for the newspaper. He was glad for her assistance because he found it very difficult. When he dictated the line "She is survived by her daughter, Alexandra Elizabeth Robinson-Parnell," he felt a lump in his throat. Sandy was too young to be mentioned in an obituary as the daughter of the deceased. It was a sad turn of fate.

When they were done, Nathalie turned to Bryce and said, "We had a call from Patty while you were at the house. She was asking if she could include some personal touches for the wake and for the funeral, you know, like putting together some pictures, and maybe telling Father Jeff some nice memories about Susan that he could include in the eulogy."

Bryce was thunderstruck by the idea. Patty had driven Susan to an early grave, and now she wanted to involve herself in the funeral as though the deceased was a loved one?

"Absolutely not," Bryce said.

"I understand how you feel," Nathalie said, "But you have to think of Sandy. We both do. We're her godparents. What impression do you think it will give people if they come to the wake or funeral and see that Patty's been forbidden to take part, and that the family is shutting her out? If it were just her, it might be a different matter, but I don't think you want people seeing that Sandy is in the midst of a chaotic situation. It's unbefitting. People know Susan and Patty were estranged, so showing that the family is united despite any marital rift will go a long way towards making things feel harmonious. For Sandy's sake," she reiterated.

Bryce had to admit she had a point. Anything the Parnells did to shun Patty would demonstrate that the family was embroiled in a raging feud. Bryce didn't care about his own reputation, but he didn't want people thinking of Sandy as a girl whose family was embittered over an ugly divorce. He didn't want any scandals following her into grade school. People had long memories where family unpleasantness was concerned.

"Okay," he said, "But I don't want to speak to her."

"No worries," Nathalie said. "I'll handle everything."

"And I'm not having her at the first night of the wake. She comes the second night, with friends and colleagues," he said. He was outraged at the thought of her being included among the first viewers, who were family-only.

Back in Connecticut later that afternoon, Bryce placed calls to his friends to notify them of Susan's death. He was awed by the outpouring of support they offered. Everyone had been shocked, and he was touched that Topher had even wept upon hearing the news.

"She was like a second big sister to me," he said.

Bryce was most shocked by Cristina's reaction, as she said she would be attending the funeral.

"Really, there's no need," he told her. He knew it was a long flight from Europe.

"Bryce, I'm coming," she said.

"I'll have someone meet you at the airport," he said.

"Don't be silly. I'll stay with Princess Solange. She's there now for a charity ball," Cristina explained.

Princess Solange was a friend of Cristina's, a minor royal from some obscure principality in Europe. She had an apartment in the city, one of her many global residences.

After he got off the phone with Cristina, he received a call from Rohan's mother in India. Even though it was some ungodly hour there, Rohan had thought it worth waking them to relay the sad news following Bryce's call. She said she wanted to personally convey condolences on behalf of herself and Rohan's father, and to tell Bryce that she would do pujas for his family.

"We are feeling for you very deeply at this time," she said, and invited him to come and stay at their estate for an extended visit when everything was over. He was touched by her kindness.

Deek, upon hearing the news, said he was coming over straightaway, but Bryce told him he preferred some privacy for a while. He hadn't been alone since the incident. Tiffany was called to the phone to offer a word of sympathy to Bryce before Deek hung up.

"That sucks," she simply said.

As it was nearing dinnertime, Bryce knew he'd have to make a call he was dreading: Uncle Clement.

Ingrid had offered to do it, but as much as he wanted to relegate the task, it was his place to inform the eldest member of the Parnell family himself.

Lupe, the maid, answered the phone and Bryce identified himself, saying he'd like to speak with Clement. She got away from him before he could ask her to stick around in case he took the news badly. A moment later, Aunt Fluff spoke.

"Hello, Bryce," she said. "To what do I owe the pleasure of your call?

"Actually, I need to speak with Uncle Clement for a moment," he said.

"About what?" she asked. She was being an annoying gatekeeper, as usual. Bryce couldn't stand that about her.

"It's a family matter," he said dismissively. "Just something I have to tell him. Is he available?"

"What kind of family matter?" she asked.

"If you must know, I have to relay some bad news," he said.

"Bad news?" she repeated. "Has something happened to the baby?"

Bryce had no idea how she concluded that, but in the background, she could hear him telling Uncle Clement, "Clement! I think something's happened to the baby."

Bryce was becoming furious. He didn't have much tolerance for her under good conditions, and much less in his current state.

"Aunt Fluff," he began.

"If anything has happened to the baby, your uncle and I will do whatever we can for Patty and Susan, but please let them know that we don't want to get involved financially. We have our future to think about," she said.

"What are you talking about?" Bryce said.

"If the real mother has come back to take the baby away. We were expecting this. We knew it would only be a matter of time," she said.

Bryce was practically shaking with anger.

"Aunt Fluff, please stop interfering. I need to speak with Uncle Clement. Please put him on the phone," he said in as steady a voice as he could manage.

Aunt Fluff made a "Hmph!" sound and said, "Well, all right then," in a frosty tone. As she passed the receiver to Uncle Clement, he heard her mumble something about him being "in quite a snit."

"Bryce? This is your Uncle Clement," Uncle Clement said. "You say there's some bad news?"

Despite Uncle Clement's age and deteriorating health, he sounded very stable and ready to face whatever was coming his way. Bryce realized that great men like his grandfather and Uncle Clement had withstood so many harsh blows over the years that they had developed a knack for remaining in control no matter what.

"Are you able to sit down?" Bryce said. "It's a rather long story," he lied, "so I don't want you to be uncomfortable."

"I'm just fine, Bryce," Uncle Clement said. "What's the matter?"

"This afternoon, Susan had a heart attack. She didn't survive," Bryce said.

"I see," Uncle Clement said.

Bryce could hear Aunt Fluff whispering "What is it? What is it?"

"Susan," he heard Uncle Clement tell her. "Susan is dead."

Bryce pitied the fact that Uncle Clement had to hear the news in the company of such an annoying person. If Bryce were there, he would've throttled Aunt Fluff.

"Okay," said Uncle Clement, returning to the phone. "Do you need any help with the arrangements?"

"No, thank you," Bryce said. "Ingrid Masterson has been taking care of everything."

"Did you call Seth?" he asked.

"Yes, I told him yesterday," Bryce said.

"Very good," Uncle Clement said. He was as composed and matter-of-fact about everything as if he were making dinner reservations at a restaurant.

"Where did it happen?" Uncle Clement asked.

"She was at home. Margaret was with her. She called the paramedics immediately, but it was too late," Bryce explained.

"That's too bad," Uncle Clement said. "Have you told Patty?"

"Yes, she knows," Bryce said.

"Now it's not for me to say," Uncle Clement began, "But if I were you, I would make Patty feel welcome to attend the funeral, assuming she wants to. There's no need to make a bad situation worse by using this as an opportunity to settle any scores. In the future, little Alexandra is going to have to live with the choices the family makes today, so that's something to bear in mind."

Bryce was glad Nathalie had talked him into allowing Patty to the wake and funeral.

"We've already extended that invitation, Uncle Clement," Bryce said. "We didn't want to create a scandal."

"That's very wise," Uncle Clement said. "Well, if you'll excuse me now, I must go, but I'm very sorry for you, Bryce. That's a terrible thing, to lose your sister."

"Thank you, Uncle Clement," Bryce said. "We'll keep you informed of the details."

Although the call was over, Uncle Clement didn't realize he hadn't properly hung up the phone, and Bryce discovered the reason he'd cut the call so short when he did: Uncle Clement was blubbering like a child.

"There, there," he heard Aunt Fluff saying tenderly, and then Lupe, or someone, finally placed the receiver back in the cradle.

Poor Uncle Clement, Bryce thought.

Aunt Fluff wasn't much, but at least she was better than nothing.

27

Bryce was now into his third day of bereavement and he was adjusting. The worst part of the day was the first few seconds of consciousness in the morning, as he invariably forgot Susan was dead, and then it hit him all at once.

He forced himself to eat at regular mealtimes whether he was hungry or not, although occasionally he was famished.

He discovered he said "Thank you" more times than he could count, because someone was always doing something for him.

And he was growing tired of hearing the word "sorry." Everyone was sorry.

It was Tuesday and the obituary was going to appear in the paper, meaning a broad circle of people were going to find out about Susan's death. That evening was going to be the first night of the wake.

When he entered the funeral home, he was greeted by the director, whom he'd met the previous day. Nathalie and Ingrid were already there, and Ben would be over shortly.

"Bryce," Natalie said, giving him a hug and taking his hand. "Would you like to see her?"

It wasn't so much a question as it was a prelude to the fact that he was being led, gently but purposefully, to his sister's coffin.

It seemed to take forever to get there, but when he did, Bryce looked at Susan. She was peaceful and her features were softened by the mortician's paraffin so that she looked like the relics of saints he'd seen in European cathedrals. She was wearing lipstick, something she never did in life, but it was a pale shade and it suited her.

Nathalie had retreated to allow him privacy. Bryce stood for a moment. His mind was blank. For once in his life, he couldn't think of anything at all.

He thought he heard Nathalie sniffling in the background, and then a moment later, he felt Ingrid's arm around him.

"I chose her powder blue dress," she was saying softly. "She bought it for Sandy's christening and she told me how much she liked the way it looked on her."

Bryce noticed Susan's diamond stud earrings. Those had been a present from their father. Bryce didn't want them buried with her.

"Her earrings," he said gesturing towards her face.

"That's only for now," Ingrid explained. "We'll remove them before the funeral."

Bryce stood silently with Ingrid for about a minute, and then he turned to have a seat. Nathalie handed him a paper cup of water, which he drank. Suddenly, he was very thirsty.

"Look at all the beautiful flowers she's received," she said.

The room was brimming with floral arrangements. He saw his own wreath at the head of the casket, arrayed with dark purple blooms. It was one of about two dozen flanking the coffin. There were large baskets and bouquets everywhere. Rohan's family had sent a veritable mountain of chrysanthemums.

"What shall we do with them all?" Bryce asked.

"We'll be taking some back to the house for the reception, and the rest will be donated to hospital patients," she explained.

That made him feel better, knowing that someone might be cheered up by them after all this was over.

"Father Jeff is coming by later," Nathalie said. "He'll be saying a few words."

Bryce heard voices by the entrance as relatives began arriving.

Aris and Loretta Jorgensen were greeted by Ingrid. Nathalie went to say hello to them and Bryce figured he should probably join her. They expressed their condolences and made their way to the casket. Soon afterwards, Aunt Bitsy appeared. Like Ingrid, Nathalie, and Ben, she'd become an honorary family member. Bryce was glad to see her. Ben arrived next, and came to join Bryce and Nathalie.

Before long, the room was filled with people. A few of his distant relatives had shown up, such as Cousin Tad, who lived in Bedford, New York with his elderly mother, Cousin Edith. She was with him. She was using a walker, but she said she could still get around fairly well. A woman Bryce vaguely recognized introduced herself as Cousin Sarah Hockney from Saddle River, New Jersey. With her were her husband Charles and her two teenage children, Tinsley and John Foster. Cousin Sarah said the last time she'd seen Bryce, he was in high school. Bryce was surprised to see the arrival of Cousin Meredith, whose family were kin to the Parnells. She lived way out on Martha's Vineyard off Cape Cod, but said she was staying with a great-nephew and his family in Millbrook, New York.

Finally, Uncle Clement arrived. Bryce's heart went out to the old man. Uncle Clement went quietly to the casket and stood for a long time. Bryce saw him wipe his face a few times. Then he coughed and straightened his jacket and turned to face the gathering.

"Bryce," he said, offering his hand.

"Hello, Uncle Clement," Bryce said. "I'm glad to see you."

Bryce greeted Aunt Fluff also. She was a bit cool to him and went to chat with the Jorgensens.

Uncle Clement sat down next to Bryce.

"My knees are starting to go," he said.

"We received some very nice flowers," Bryce said.

"Yes, I see that," Uncle Clement said. "You also got some Mass cards."

"Did we?" Bryce asked.

"Yes. She must've known a lot of Catholics," he commented.

"There are the Ryans, but I can't think of anyone else," Bryce said.

"There must be more. There are several Mass cards out there," he said, indicating one of the anterooms. "People are going to think she was a nun."

Bryce laughed.

When he took a look later, he saw that there was a Mass card from Monsignor Ryan and his wife, Marguerite. There were also Mass cards from both Margaret and John, which Bryce thought was a lovely gesture. Uncle Clement had exaggerated about how many there were, but then again, he wasn't particularly fond of Catholics.

Father Jeff showed up around 8:30PM and everyone assembled in the viewing room. He said that he was glad to have some time alone with the family and shared a few memories of Susan. Then he read a passage from the Book of Psalms and invited everyone to join him in a prayer. Before he left, he came and sat with Bryce for a while.

"How's it going?" he asked.

"It's going fine," Bryce said.

"Glad to hear it. Can I tell you a little secret?" Father Jeff asked.

"What's that?" Bryce asked.

"I've noticed that weddings and funerals bring out the worst in people. Now I'm not asking you to name names, but can you confirm for me that there's at least one person in this room right now that you'd like to strangle?" he asked.

Bryce laughed. "As a matter of fact, there is."

"Good, good," Father Jeff said, nodding. "Because if you told me there wasn't at least one person, then either my observation's wrong or you're not trying hard enough, and I don't like to be wrong."

"Is everything set for the funeral?" Bryce asked.

"Yes. We are ready," Father Jeff said. "The music director has some really nice selections picked out and we have a soloist who'll be singing. We're expecting a big crowd, but I can promise that seating isn't going to be an issue for you."

Bryce smiled. "Thanks," he said.

"Any time," Father Jeff said, and then he left.

On the following evening, the second night of the wake was much like the first except there were many more people, and someone had pinned a heart-shaped floral arrangement inside the coffin lid with a ribbon which read "Mother." It was from Sandy.

On this night, Bryce had to receive the visitors, and he was fortunate to have Aunt Bitsy beside him to remind him who everyone was.

As two young women approached, Aunt Bitsy whispered, "Those are the Taylor girls. Their mother was an acquaintance of your mother. They're part of the horsey set," and when a tall gentleman wearing an expensive suit appeared, she quietly said, "That's Oswald White. He's with a bank your father used to do business with."

A few of Bryce's friends showed up, including Deek and Tiffany. They were glad to see he was holding up well. Indeed, as the days went on, Bryce felt it got easier.

"You know the thing I felt at the hospital gala? This was it," Tiffany said.

Just then, Rosemary and Topher arrived. Juliette was with Topher, so Bryce finally had a chance to meet her. She seemed very nice, but Bryce noticed she adopted that pseudo-spiritual tone that many snotty rich people did in order to seem humble and enlightened. Everything she said was kind of whispery, as if she were leading a yoga class.

“It’s wonderful that so many people have come to pay their respects,” Rosemary said.

“Yes,” Topher agreed. “I didn’t realize Susan even knew this many people.”

“This is the kind of memory you treasure,” Juliette said in her dreamy voice.

Bryce didn’t think there was anything to treasure about being forced to remain in a room with his sister’s body while having to meet hundreds of strangers, but he let it go. He remembered what Father Jeff had said.

There was a buzz that seemed to be going around the room. People were turning to look at the entrance. Bryce looked too, and saw Patty, escorted by one of her brothers. Suddenly, everyone seemed to look at Bryce.

Without hesitation, he made his way through the crowd until he reached her. He put his arms out and Patty clutched him wordlessly in a hug that went on for much longer than it should have, Bryce thought.

“Bryce,” she whined, starting to cry, “I don’t think I can do this.”

“I’ll help you,” he said. Her brother nodded to Bryce, and Bryce took her arm. They walked to the coffin.

“The flowers from Sandy are lovely,” he said as they approached. He was hoping they might distract her and lessen the shock of seeing Susan.

Patty remained steady when they arrived. He went to release her so she could have a moment alone, but she clutched at his arm.

“Don’t leave me,” she whispered, not taking her eyes off Susan. She stood, taking it all in and crying wordlessly, and then signaled to Bryce that she wanted to be taken back. He returned her to her brother. Bryce still didn’t remember his name. Joseph? Jonathan? Jerome? All three of her brother’s names started with “J.”

Several friends of Patty’s had come, and now they congregated around her. In no time at all, the funeral parlor was effectively divided into two neat camps, Susan’s people on one side and Patty and her supporters on the other.

Bryce needed a breath of air. It was freezing outside, but the cold would do him good. The funeral director was only too happy to show him a private side entrance, outside of which he would be undisturbed. Mourners at funeral homes frequently needed special assistance, whether it be a quiet place to get away from everyone or a clandestine shot of whiskey. The funeral directors had seen it all and were compassionate about helping.

Once outside, he drew a deep breath. He wasn’t sure how he felt about having openly acknowledged Patty, but it was over. There would be no scandal. That was the most important thing.

However, he had been shocked by how fragile she was. She looked like a wreck. As she beheld her wife's lifeless body, he got the impression she was horrified by what she'd done. In one sense, he felt that was probably punishment enough.

At the end of the evening, Patty approached him and they went to talk alone quietly in a side room.

"Bryce, I don't even know how to begin," she said. "I can apologize, I can tell you how awful I feel, I can tell you that the doctors had to give me tranquilizing injections, but none of that will bring Susan back."

"Susan was sorry for everything that had happened," Bryce reminded her. "You were the one who wanted to leave."

"Yes," she said, "But I had felt for a very long time that—"

Bryce cut her off. "I am not going to sit here and listen to you justifying your selfish, vengeful behavior, because that's what it was. You did everything you could to hurt her. You broke her heart. You killed her," he said angrily.

Patty looked like she was going to throw up. She covered her mouth and nose with her handkerchief.

Once she had composed herself, she quietly said, "She was always unreasonable with me. Everything had to be her way. You know that."

"Then if that's how it was, you leave. You don't get your lawyers to punish her and tell her she's never going to see her daughter again," Bryce spat.

"This is hard for me," she said. "Please don't think that I don't feel anything for her, because I do. And you're right, I was angry. I wanted to let her feel weak and powerless for a change. My family even tried to talk me out of it, that's how blind with rage I was."

"But you're the last person on earth I ever expected would do such a thing," Bryce said. "I loved you. I trusted you."

"I still love you," she said, "But I understand how you might feel about me now. And that's okay. I have to move forward. We all have to move forward. Sometimes saying things like this is what has to happen to make that possible."

Bryce realized he was tearing up because he ached to feel close to her but he was still very angry. It was a strange combination of emotions that he'd never experienced before.

Bryce took a deep breath. "I don't think this is anything we can solve in one sitting, but maybe we can reach a détente."

"'Not enemies'?" Patty suggested.

"Not enemies," Bryce agreed.

28

Late into the night, a giant stormfront moved in. By morning, the rain was coming down in sheets.

Bryce hoped it wouldn't be as bad in New York, but it was worse. He could barely see well enough to drive to the funeral.

When he arrived at the church, the rain was coming down in torrents. His umbrella did little to protect him, and by the time he entered the sanctuary, he was cold and wet.

He took his place at the front of the church, feeling chilled. In time, the rest of the family arrived. Patty sat towards the front on the other side of the church. Her brother sat on one side of her and Gabe sat on the other. For once, he wasn't wearing sunglasses. However, Patty wore a black veil, which Bryce thought was highly inappropriate. In his mind, while they were technically still married at the time of Susan's death, they were legally separated, and she had no right to don the traditional symbol of widowhood.

The church quickly filled up and the Mass began. Father Jeff was somber and eloquent. Nathalie did a reading from the Bible. The soloist performed a particularly moving rendition of Mendelsohn's "O, For the Wings of a Dove." Bryce could hear sniffles among the congregation.

Finally, it was time to carry the casket. Bryce took his place with the other pallbearers. Despite his age, Uncle Clement insisted on performing his duty, so he and Bryce led at the front. Behind them were Aris Jorgensen and Monsignor Ryan, and at the back were Deek and Ben.

Bryce was heavy-hearted, but he stood tall, knowing that this was the moment when he owed Susan his very best. As they processed up the aisle, it was painful to see the many sad faces in the crowd, but a few stood out: Ingrid, who had attended her husband's funeral less than a year ago at that same church, Aunt Bitsy, who looked positively stricken, and Rohan, with tears streaming down his face.

The men walked out into the pouring rain and placed the casket into the hearse.

Bryce had never been so miserable in all his life.

Few people proceeded on to the graveside service, preferring instead to go directly to the reception, but Bryce was glad. He didn't think Susan would've wanted a lot of people staring down into her grave.

Mindful of the weather, Father Jeff kept things very brief. Then someone handed Bryce a rose and motioned for him to toss it atop the coffin. Despite the incessant drone of rain falling on the tarp that covered the gravesite, he heard someone sobbing loudly. He turned to look.

It was Patty. She was standing towards the back of the gathering. He had a pretty good idea that she was not being included in the flower ceremony, so he beckoned to her and she came forward.

He put his arm around her and handed her the rose. She was shivering. She released it into the grave and looked at Bryce.

"Thank you," she said through her tears.

When everything was finished, he walked to his car. As he opened the door, Patty ran to meet him.

"Bryce," she called loudly.

She didn't have an umbrella, so her hair was sodden, and straggles of it stuck to the sides of her face. Her coat was soaking wet. Her mascara was running. She looked like a madwoman.

When she came to him, he held his umbrella over her.

"Here," she said, fumbling in her purse for something.

She handed him a heavy gold ring.

"This was Grandfather Parnell's signet ring," she said. "You should take it."

Bryce looked at it and recalled that Grandfather had given it to Susan shortly before he died.

"Susan gave it to me one time after we had a fight, but it's family jewelry. You should have it," she explained.

"Thanks," Bryce said, putting the ring in his pocket. "Is it okay if I come and visit Sandy sometimes?" he asked.

"Yes," Patty said enthusiastically. "I want you to be part of her life."

With that, she threw her arms around him and gave him a big hug. They were both drenched, but Bryce felt warm inside for the first time since Susan's death.

"Come back to the house with me," he said.

"No," she said, turning. "I'm going home. That's where I belong."

"Talk soon?" Bryce asked.

"Yes. Take care," Patty said.

"You too," Bryce said.

29

As soon as Bryce reached the house, he went upstairs to change. He felt like a giant sponge. Every bit of clothing on him was soaked.

Downstairs, Margaret, Polly, and John had everything running smoothly. Bryce had to admit, sad though it was to say, it was probably the best reception that had ever been given in that house. The flowers were magnificent, the crystal and silver were sparkling, and Bryce had never seen such a lovely buffet in his life.

Everyone was grateful for the strong hot coffee Margaret served, and people were talking and laughing. Susan would've wanted it that way.

Cristina came up to him and gave him a big hug. Bryce was surprised. He'd forgotten all about her.

"I was sitting right behind you in church, didn't you see me?" she asked.

"How was your trip?" Bryce asked.

"Very nice," she said. "The Mass was lovely."

"Yes, wasn't it?" he said.

"That singer—what a voice," Cristina said, adding, "I love the priest. He's too cute. I wanted to eat him up."

"Father Jeff? Yes, he's really something. Very down-to-earth guy," Bryce said.

"He's absolutely adorable. I want to stuff him in my luggage and take him home. You don't think he does private spiritual counseling to lonely wives on the Italian Riviera, do you?" she asked.

"You can ask him yourself," Bryce said. "He's right over there."

"You think I'm kidding," she said after him as Bryce went to speak with Rohan.

"Bryce, I am so sorry," Rohan said, embracing him warmly.

"This week has been hellish," Bryce admitted.

"There is something I want to share with you," Rohan said. "It's a quote by Tagore: 'Death is not extinguishing the light; it is only putting out the lamp because the dawn has come.'"

"That's a beautiful thought," Bryce said. "And thank you very much for the flowers. I was really touched by your family's kindness."

"That's nothing. Really, you should see what we do in India," Rohan told him.

"I might get to find out. Your mother invited me to visit," Bryce said.

"Yes, by all means! You must come. They miss you," Rohan said.

"Excuse me," Bryce said, spotting Uncle Clement. "I'll swing back later but there's someone I have to talk to."

"Uncle Clement," Bryce said when he had reached him, "Do you need a change of clothes? I don't want you to catch cold."

"No, I'm fine," Uncle Clement said, "We're not staying long. It's been a hard day."

"I understand," Bryce said. "I came over because I wanted to tell you how much it meant to me that you were there today, and that you served as a pallbearer."

"I was only doing my duty," Uncle Clement said.

"Susan had great respect for you. We all know how much she loved Grandfather, but I'm pretty sure you were a close second," Bryce said.

"Well, she was very dear to me," Uncle Clement said. "You both are. I never told you this, but you remind me a lot of Woodrow when he was a boy."

"You mean he was once as flighty as I am?" Bryce asked.

"Woodrow? Never. He was investing in real estate when he was seven years old," Uncle Clement said. "I mean you look like him."

"Oh," Bryce said.

"Where you get your personality from is anyone's guess," Uncle Clement said.

Polly came by with a tray and offered Uncle Clement a finger sandwich.

Bryce went to thank several other people who'd been instrumental in helping him not lose his mind, including Deek and Tiffany.

Good old Deek, I can always count on him, Bryce thought.

"This is a really nice house," Tiffany said.

"Thank you," Bryce said.

"I could see living someplace like this," she said. "Deek's been talking about us living down in Banjoland after we get married, but I like it up here."

"But that's my family estate. That's where it is, so that's where I'll have to be," Deek said.

"You've got money. Just move the house up here," Tiffany suggested.

"It doesn't work that way," Bryce said. "Deek will explain."

Bryce was on his way towards the kitchen to see how Margaret was doing when he spotted Stephanie.

"Hi, I didn't realize you were here," he said.

"I was hiding in the back of the church," she said. "I know there's been some talk about me so I didn't want to—you know."

"Oh, who cares?" Bryce said. "Life's too short."

Polly appeared with a tray of crackers topped with deviled chicken. Stephanie took one.

"How are you feeling?" Bryce asked.

"Good," she said, nodding. She'd taken a bite of the hors d'oeuvre and some of the cracker was falling out of the corner of her mouth. That always happened when she ate. Bryce found it morbidly fascinating.

“What are you doing for Christmas?” he asked.

“I’m going to my parents’,” she said.

“Why don’t you come with me to the Masterson’s?” he said.

“Are you sure?” she asked.

“Yes,” he said.

Stephanie mentioned that Topher and Juliette were heading their way.

“Have you met her?” Bryce asked.

“Yes. She’s nice, but she talks in this really phony spiritual way,” Stephanie said.

“You think so too?” Bryce asked, laughing.

Bryce said hello to Topher and Juliette and thanked them for coming, then he stole off to the kitchen.

Margaret seemed glad to see him.

“I heard it was a nice funeral,” she said.

“Yes. So many people showed up,” Bryce said.

“Is there anything you wanted?” she asked.

“No, I just came to let you know how much Mother and Susan appreciated you. I don’t know what we’d do without you,” Bryce said.

Bryce thought he saw Margaret’s lip quiver but she didn’t become emotional.

“Working for someone like your sister was a pleasure,” Margaret said. “She was a real lady. Not many of those around any more these days.”

“Things are apt to be busy with Christmas coming up and I have a lot of legal matters to sort out,” Bryce said, “but if I don’t have a chance to talk to you before you start at the Masterson’s, please know how grateful my family has been for everything.”

“You’re more than welcome,” Margaret said.

Bryce returned to the reception feeling proud of himself. He’d survived the wake and funeral, and with significant help from Ingrid and Nathalie, was hosting a reception worthy of the Parnells. He was emotionally drained, and somewhere in his heart there was still a gaping wound, but for once, he felt a sense of deep satisfaction.

30

The following day, Bryce drank copious amounts of tea and hot consommé. He’d taken a bit of a chill at the funeral and didn’t want to be sick for Christmas. Ingrid had enthusiastically agreed to let him bring Stephanie for dinner and he was looking forward to it.

Now that the funeral was over, Seth called, as he anticipated. They discussed Susan's will. Bryce's lawyer, Michael, would work through the particulars, but Seth wanted to give him a general rundown.

Susan had recently revised her will in light of her impending divorce. Given that Patty had custody of Sandy at the time and might be expected to retain sole custody, Sandy chose to leave everything to Bryce rather than Sandy. However, Seth said that Susan would surely have wanted Sandy to have an inheritance. Basically speaking, this meant that Bryce could reasonably expect to keep Susan's money, since Patty's family had plenty of that to give her, but that anything with intrinsic value, such as the house in Tuxedo Park, should eventually be given to Sandy once she attained majority.

Bryce figured that was a good deal. It would be seventeen years before he had to turn the house over to her.

That afternoon, he had an appointment with Father Jeff.

"I meant to tell you," the priest said when Bryce sat down in his office, "That was one of the best attended Masses we've ever had. I think that says a lot about a person."

"I wonder if I could make a large donation to the church in memory of Susan," Bryce said. "I happen to know that your sermon on Sunday morning brought a lot of comfort to her. Knowing that she had some happy moments that day is a great comfort to me now."

"Of course, but let's talk about that later. Speaking of that day," Father Jeff said, "It hasn't even been a week. You've barely had a chance to perform on any of the seven glorious stages of grief. How are you holding up?"

"A lot of my anger at Patty is gone," Bryce said. "During the wake and funeral, I could see that she's the only other person on the planet who feels the pain as badly as I do. We were the two people who loved Susan the most."

"Astute observation," Father Jeff said. "And speaking from experience, you can't go wrong with the forgiveness thing. Jesus only mentioned it a couple dozen times, but I believe eventually he would've gotten around to seriously promoting it."

Bryce laughed.

"That's the thing about love," Father Jeff said. "It expands. Fear contracts us, but love always opens us up."

"I suppose I do let fear linger in my thoughts," Bryce said.

"What are you afraid of?" Father Jeff asked.

Bryce thought a moment. "The first thing that comes to mind is actually something that came up during a socio-political conversation I had with a friend."

"Go on," Father Jeff said. "Sounds interesting."

Bryce was a little embarrassed. “I hope this doesn’t sound snobbish, but we were discussing the fate of rich old families like ours, and he told me about powerful interests that were really running the world, sifting out our kind and exploiting the poor like dumb sheep, just like it says in the Bible.”

“And that worried you?” Father Jeff asked.

“It’s pretty depressing to think there isn’t much of a future for us all, because some major players are the ones who are running the show,” Bryce said.

“Bryce,” Father Jeff said flatly, “You realize you’re talking to a priest, right? I know who’s running the show, and it isn’t these dastardly villains you’re talking about. Care to take a guess who is?”

“God?” Bryce said.

“Right,” Father Jeff said. “Now repeat after me, ‘God is running the show.’ If you’re not convinced, let’s get a committee together to handle making the sun rise every day. Think we could manage that? Hah! We can barely pull off a Superbowl halftime show.”

“But these forces are out to use and abuse others,” Bryce said.

“Yeah? Well, what are you going to do about it?” Father Jeff asked. “You started a nonprofit. You’re fighting the good fight. That’s what you do, Bryce. That’s the gamechanger.”

“I guess you’re right,” Bryce conceded. “This person I was talking with, he also had an important point about how the powerful are afraid of radicals, but really, the fact that they buy into their own myth is what brings them down and ultimately proves they aren’t as powerful as they think. What was it he said? It’s ‘the nemesis of the great.’”

“I’m highly inclined to agree,” Father Jeff said. “In fact, if you’re as much of a religion nerd as I am, you know that Nemesis was a Greek goddess.”

“No, I didn’t know that,” Bryce said.

“Yes,” Father Jeff said. “If things don’t work out for me here, I’m on the next boat to Athens. Nemesis brought bad karma down on the proud—those who were arrogant before the gods.”

“So what’s our role in all that?” Bryce asked.

“Seriously? Whenever you’re in doubt, throw love at it. That’s the greatest weapon we’ve got. It can be slow-acting compared to, say, napalm, but it gets the job done.”

Bryce was glad to have talked with Father Jeff. Even though he was completely bewildered about much of what they discussed, he felt he was moving in the right direction. It occurred to him that getting one’s spiritual bearings didn’t happen all at once, like receiving an itinerary for a trip. Much of the decision-making was done on the fly.

Overall, Bryce realized there was more to God than he could possibly imagine, and the thought gladdened him.

Two days later, he and Stephanie had Christmas dinner at the Masterson's. They had a very nice time, and everyone spoke about Susan, so it almost felt as if she were there. Nathalie and Ben announced that they were expecting a baby, which made everyone very happy.

Bryce and Stephanie spent New Year's Eve together and decided to resume their relationship. A lot of things had changed over the years, and they felt they were finally in the right place for each other. On St. Valentine's Day, they became engaged to be married.

Meanwhile, Rosemary finally gave up on David. She decided she was probably best suited to single life, anyway. Meanwhile, Topher and Juliette continued to date and to support each other in their sobriety.

In the spring, Uncle Clement died. Standing at his grave, Bryce felt a greater sense of gratitude than loss. Uncle Clement had been the real grandfather-figure in his life, with his wise advice and brusque affection. With no small astonishment at the workings of fate, Bryce realized that he himself was now the head of the Parnell family. Ironically, Grandfather had overlooked and underestimated him, never knowing he would ultimately be the one to perpetuate their legacy.

Patty and Sandy came up to visit, and Bryce was amazed at how much his goddaughter had grown. His relationship with Patty continued to heal, and he was pleased that she was getting back into photography. As for Gabe, he and Bryce continued to associate, and Bryce found him to be a unique and valuable resource as well as a genuine friend.

By summer, Rohan announced that his parents had found him a wonderful match, and he was ecstatic. Bryce and Stephanie made plans to travel to India for an extended vacation.

As summer unfolded into autumn, Bryce felt he was reclaiming his life. So much of the past few months had been steeped in grief, it was freeing to think that finally, his thoughts about Susan were more often uplifting than sad.

Fortunately, his nonprofit was succeeding steadily and he found fulfillment in his work, but it was quickly becoming clear that changes were occurring that would bring about a new world.

Bryce had been running. Between the establishment of his charitable organization and his study of spiritual principles, he was doing everything he could to recreate himself in such a way that he could both survive the future and help as many others as possible.

One quiet night in his cabin, Bryce sat by the fire, holding Grandfather's signet ring. He looked at it for a long time before putting it on his finger.

It fit perfectly.

The next morning, he rose and looked out the window. The sun was streaming in.

He knew he could not change the past, and he knew he could not be anything other than what he was.

And with that, Bryce set out to find his place in the world.

THE END

About the Author

Born in Manhattan and raised in Texas, Cinzi Lavin is an award-winning writer-composer known for her "Nantasket Trilogy" of musical dramas about the seaside town of Hull, Massachusetts. She has professional experience as an actress, singer, instrumentalist, and educator, and her career highlights include a performance by invitation at the White House. She and her husband make their home in Litchfield County, Connecticut.

www.ingramcontent.com/pod-product-compliance
Lightning Source LLC
LaVergne TN
LVHW091009080826
845145LV00003B/1196

9781736635018

To the ones who manage, remember, and carry it all.

To the invisible effort that keeps things running,
and the expectations that are rarely spoken out loud.

To the exhaustion that can exist
even when everything is getting done.

May you be met with gentleness.
May your effort be honored, even in silence.
May you find small pockets of rest that belong only to you.

With Googolplex Love,

MommyHooray ♡

MommyHooray Presents: Invisible Burnout
by MommyHooray

Written and published under the pen name MommyHooray.
Illustrations created using digital illustration tools.

Printed in the United States of America.

ISBN: 978-1-972071-44-1

For more stories and updates, visit:
https://sites.google.com/view/mommyhooray

MommyHooray Presents:

Invisible Burnout

The Silence of Carrying Too Much

by MommyHooray

♡Not all burnout is easy to see.

It blends into your everyday life,
into the way you keep going,
keep smiling,
keep showing up.

And because everything still works,
no one notices how tired you really are.
Maybe not even you.

But this kind of tiredness isn't who you are.
It's a sign you've been carrying too much
for too long.

You wake up already tired.

Not because you didn't sleep,
but because everything is already waiting for you
before you've even had a moment to arrive.

Your mind starts moving
before your feet touch the floor.

And somehow,
you're already behind.

I wake up tired.
M
7:00
lunch
dishes
laundry
emails
appointments
groceries

You don't stop.

Not because you can't,
but because stopping feels like things will unravel.
So you keep going,
holding it all together as best you can.

And even in that,
there's a strength in you—
the kind that keeps showing up,
even when you need a moment too.

If I stop,
everything
falls.
M

You remember everything—
appointments, deadlines,
what everyone needs before they even ask.

It all lives with you,
held quietly,
kept in motion.

And even when no one notices what you carry,
you still do.

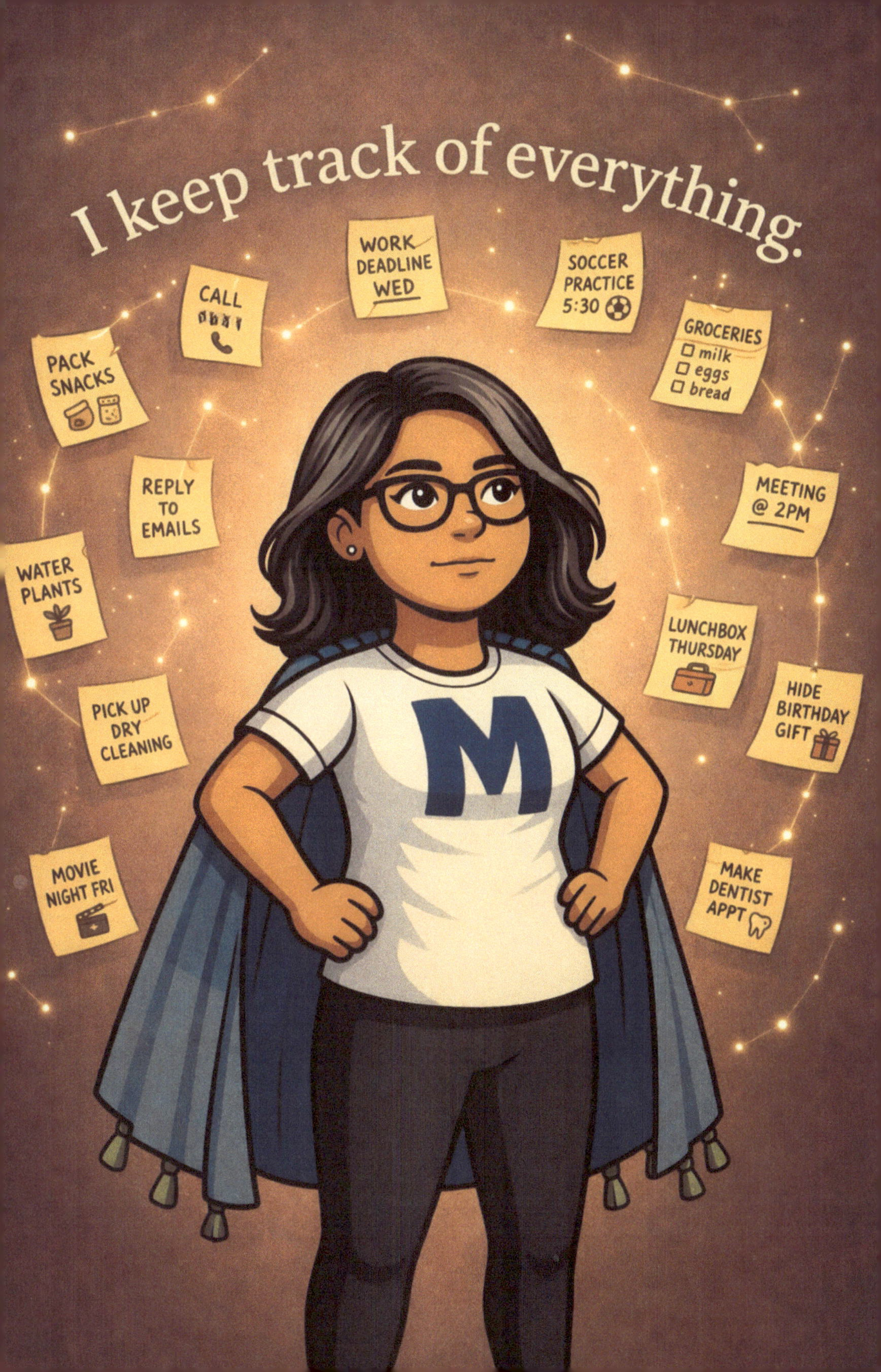
I keep track of everything.
WORK DEADLINE WED
SOCCER PRACTICE 5:30
CALL
GROCERIES
milk
eggs
bread
PACK SNACKS
REPLY TO EMAILS
MEETING @ 2PM
WATER PLANTS
LUNCHBOX THURSDAY
PICK UP DRY CLEANING
HIDE BIRTHDAY GIFT
MOVIE NIGHT FRI
MAKE DENTIST APPT

You say, “I’m fine,”
because explaining feels heavier
than just carrying it.

So you hold it in,
keep things moving,
and make it look easy.

And somehow,
you keep showing up anyway.

I say I'm fine because it's easier.

You show up,
even on the days you wish you could disappear
for just a moment.

You still step in,
still give what you can,
still find a way to be there.

And that quiet choice
counts more than you realize.

I show up anyway.

You give the best parts of yourself away—
your patience, your energy, your attention—
offering them where they're needed most.

And somehow,
you keep going with what's left,
finding a way to make it enough
even when it doesn't feel like it is.

I give
my best
away.

You carry the mental load—
the invisible list that never stops running
in the background of your mind.

Always tracking,
always remembering,
always one step ahead.

And even when no one sees it,
it's still real...
and it still counts.

My mind never rests.

You make it look easy,
and that's why no one sees
how much it takes.

You carry it so well.
It almost disappears.

But the effort is real...
and so are you.

I make it look easy.
THURS
M

You feel guilty for being tired,
even though you never really stopped.

You've been carrying so much for so long.
It just became normal.

But that kind of tiredness deserves care too.

M
I feel guilty
for resting.

You say yes,
and then yes again,
and somehow, one more time.

You keep showing up,
stretching what you have to give,
making space where there wasn't any.

And that kind of giving means something.

Yes!
Yes!
Yes!
Yes!
Yes!
Yes!
I keep saying yes.

You carry what isn't yours,
because someone has to.

You step in where things would fall,
holding more than your share without being asked.

And even when it goes unseen,
it still matters.

I carry more than mine.

You forget what you need,
not because it doesn't matter,
but because everything else feels more urgent.

So you keep moving,
placing yourself a little further down the list
each time.

But what you need still matters too.

I forget myself.

You keep going on empty,
because stopping isn't something
you've let yourself do.

So you push through,
finding a way forward
even when there's nothing left to give.

And even that...
is a kind of strength.

I keep going anyway.

You stay light,
you stay easy,
holding things together for everyone else.

You soften the edges,
keep the mood steady,
make it all feel manageable.

And even that quiet steadiness is something real.

I keep it light
for everyone.
M

You tell yourself this is just a season,
something that will pass.

But the seasons keep repeating,
quietly folding into one another
before you've had time to rest.

And still...
you keep going.

It keeps repeating.
M

You don’t ask for help,
not because you don’t need it,
but because it feels easier to just do it yourself.

So you carry it quietly,
keeping things moving,
making it work.

And even that has its weight.

I just do it
myself.

You hold everything together,
quietly and beautifully,
in ways most people never see.

You keep it steady,
keep it moving,
keep it from falling apart.

And even when it goes unnoticed,
it still matters.

No one sees
what I hold.
M

You wonder why you feel this way,
when everything looks fine on the outside.

Nothing seems wrong,
and yet something feels heavy.

And that quiet feeling...
is worth listening to.

Why do I
feel like this?
M

You keep going,
because love looks like showing up
even when you're tired.

So you stay,
you give,
you keep choosing to be there.

And that kind of love is real.

Love keeps me going.

But even you...

were never meant to carry it all alone.

You were never meant

to hold everything together by yourself.

And needing support

doesn't take away your strength.

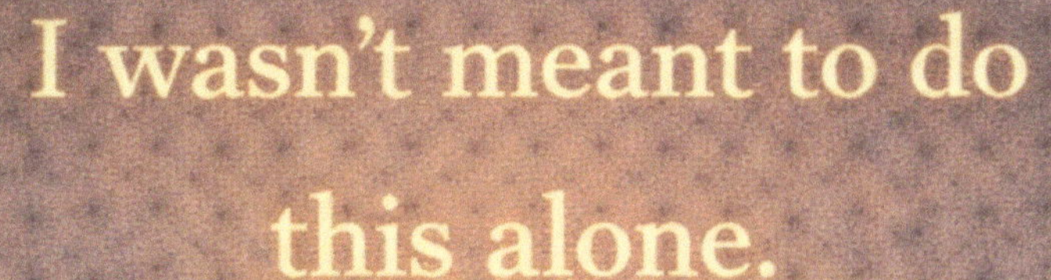
I wasn't meant to do
this alone.

Maybe strength isn't holding everything together.

Maybe it's knowing
when to set something down,
when to loosen your grip,
when to give yourself a little space to breathe.

And that kind of strength still counts.

I can put something down.

You don't have to prove you're exhausted
to deserve rest.

You don't have to earn
a moment of stillness
or push yourself any further to justify it.

You're allowed to pause,
to breathe,
to take a moment back for yourself...

Not because everything is done,
but because you matter too.

And that...
is enough. ♡

MommyHooray ♡

Also by MommyHooray

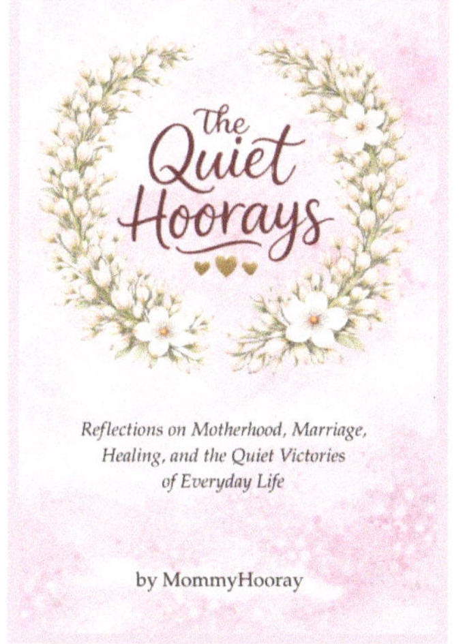

... and more!

From My Heart to Yours

Write something meaningful
for the person who will cherish this book, or for yourself.

Today's Date: ________________

May this page find you again, years from now.

www.ingramcontent.com/pod-product-compliance
Lightning Source LLC
LaVergne TN
LVHW052259100826
845147LV00001B/92

9781972071441